WEAPON

THE MP5
SUBMACHINE GUN

LEROY THOMPSON

Series Editor Martin Pegler

First published in Great Britain in 2014 by Osprey Publishing,
PO Box 883, Oxford, OX1 9PL, UK
PO Box 3985, New York, NY 10185-3985, USA
E-mail: info@ospreypublishing.com

Osprey Publishing is part of the Osprey Group

A CIP catalog record for this book is available from the British
Library

Print ISBN: 978 1 78200 917 7
PDF ebook ISBN: 978 1 78200 919 1
ePub ebook ISBN: 978 1 78200 918 4

Index by Mark Swift
Typeset in Sabon and Univers
Battlescenes by Johnny Shumate
Cutaway by Alan Gilliland
Originated by PDQ Media, Bungay, UK
Printed in China through Worldprint Ltd

14 15 16 17 18   10 9 8 7 6 5 4 3 2 1

Osprey Publishing is supporting the Woodland Trust, the UK's
leading woodland conservation charity, by funding the dedication
of trees.

www.ospreypublishing.com

Author's acknowledgments
The author would like to thank the following individuals who
helped in the preparation of this book: Paul Abbott, Ken Choate,
Jim Comparato, Gina McNeely, T.J. Mullin, US Department of
Defense.

Editor's note
Metric units of measurement are used in this book. For ease of
comparison please refer to the following conversion table:

1m = 1.09yd / 3.28ft
1cm = 0.39in
1mm = 0.04in
1kg = 2.20lb / 35.27oz
1g = 15.43 grains
1 grain = 0.06g
1m/sec = 3.28ft/sec

Front cover images are courtesy (top) author and (bottom) US
Navy. Title page image is courtesy CSSA, Inc.

CONTENTS

INTRODUCTION

Since its introduction in the 1960s, the Heckler & Koch (HK) MP5 submachine gun (SMG) has become the most widely used SMG in the world, especially among counterterrorist and special-operations units. Though widely depicted in films, on television, and in video games, the MP5 has not become quite as well recognized among the general public as weapons such as the Thompson or the Uzi. This situation may be because most of the units that use the MP5 are somewhat secretive, hence their firearms are not as well known. Unlike the Thompson or the Uzi, the MP5 also has not seen large-scale deployment on the battlefield. Its niche is more for selective and rapid elimination of the enemy on clandestine operations. Of course, the very nature of its users and missions have given it a mystique all its own, and its effectiveness has made it coveted by special forces operators the world over.

Initially known as the HK54, the MP5 was developed as part of a series of weapons with a design heritage in the HK G3 battle rifle. The HK54 employed a roller-delayed blowback action, which could easily handle the 9×19mm cartridge. From the beginning the MP5 developed a reputation for accuracy due to its free-floating hammer-forged barrel and closed-bolt operating system, among other factors. Sights, which consist of a front hooded post and rear rotary drum, aided in accuracy as well, since they were superior to most other SMG sights available. Although the MP5 normally comes with a flash suppressor, it is designed so that various other accessories – including a blank-firing training device, grenade launcher, and a suppressor – may be mounted. As with other weapons based on the G3, the receiver of the MP5 incorporates notches that allow the mounting of optical sights. As the MP5 achieved wide usage, an array of aftermarket accessories were developed, including Picatinny rails, vertical foregrips, and an array of illuminators. In the early days, however, units such as the British Special Air Service (SAS) had to develop their own methods for mounting lights and other accessories.

The two basic original versions of the MP5 were the MP5A2 with polymer fixed stock and the MP5A3 with collapsible steel stock. These remain two of the most widely used versions today. Specialized missions required specialized versions of the MP5; the shorter MP5K was developed for use by close-protection teams and others needing a concealable SMG, while the suppressed MP5SD was developed for silent elimination of the enemy or for operations in venues where muzzle flash could ignite gases or fumes. Some special-operations units have acquired versions of the MP5 tailored to their own special needs. To meet the requirements of naval special warfare (NSW) units such as the SEALs or the British Special Boat Service (SBS), in 1986, HK developed the MP5-N, sometimes termed the "Maritime Model," for use in and around salt water. Corrosion-resistant finishes and coatings were used for the parts in this version. Other units adopted versions of the MP5 in calibers other than the standard 9×19mm NATO. The US Federal Bureau of Investigation (FBI), for example, acquired the MP5 in 10mm caliber.

The MP5's accurate, potent firepower made the weapon an immediate success among counterterrorist units, for whom shot placement was absolutely critical. This accuracy and reliability, plus availability of the MP5 in the first decade after the Munich Olympics massacre of September 1972, made it the weapon of choice for most counterterrorist units formed during the 1970s and 1980s.

One of the first well-known users of the MP5 was West Germany's Grenzschutzgruppe 9 (Border Police Group 9; GSG 9) counterterrorist

One of the great advantages of the MP5 is that it offers a compact yet effective weapon that may be carried for personal protection. This member of the US Army Special Forces in Iraq carries his MP5 slung and close at hand while interacting with the locals. (US Navy)

unit. When training with GSG 9, the SAS was impressed with the MP5 and adopted it for their Special Projects (SP) Team. Its use by these two high-profile units helped popularize the MP5 with military and police special-operations groups. Reportedly, the first UK police adoption was of the MP5K, by Britain's Metropolitan Police Service ("the Met") for its Diplomatic Protection Unit, for use when guarding certain high-profile dignitaries. Semi-auto HK MP5 carbines have become the standard longarm (rifles, shotguns, or carbines) for deployment with the Met's Armed Response Vehicles (ARVs) and airport security units. These semi-auto versions are designated MP5-SFA2, the "SF" indicating "single fire." Since the MP5-SF is virtually identical to the MP5, less the parts that allow select-fire capability, it can also take the variety of accessories developed for the MP5. Many other UK police departments have also adopted the semi-auto MP5 carbine.

Versions of the MP5 are widely used among US police agencies. In the United States, the MP5, sometimes in semi-automatic versions, has replaced the shotgun in patrol cars for many law-enforcement agencies. A substantial number of those on the streets in the United States are select-fire models, especially in the hands of Special Weapons and Tactics (SWAT) teams. In some jurisdictions patrol officers have select-fire MP5s, but in other cases they use the semi-auto carbine version.

A US Marine officer firing an MP5SD, the suppressed version of the MP5. The MP5 would become so popular with military and police agencies that eventually more than 80 countries would adopt it, from Albania to Zambia. To some extent, in recent years the popularity of the MP5 has declined as units formerly using it have adopted compact rifle-caliber carbines. Nevertheless, it remains the most ubiquitous SMG in the world. (US DOD)

The broader influence of the MP5 is marked, both technically and tactically. Prior to the development of the MP5, the SMG was not normally considered a precision weapon, but the MP5 changed such thinking. The MP5's accuracy has allowed the creation of an entire system based on the MP5 for use in hostage-rescue or other precision-shooting situations. For such use the MP5 is often equipped with an optical sight and almost always with a light and/or laser. To allow units to train for close-quarters battle (CQB) with the MP5, .22-cal. conversion units have been developed, as have "Blue" versions designed to fire Simunition paint-marking cartridges.

The MP5's influence is also seen in the weapon designed by HK as its replacement – the Universal Machine Pistol (UMP) – though the MP5 remains in production. There is even a version of the UMP chambered for the .45 ACP round; in fact, the UMP was originally developed to supply the US market with a .45-cal. SMG.

The MP5 is among the most successful SMG designs since World War II, its only real competitor having been the Uzi. Though it has received quite a bit of competition from the 5.7×28mm Fabrique Nationale (FN) P90 Personal Defense Weapon (PDW) over the last 25 years, the MP5's popularity remains high. Certainly, the MP5 is *the* SMG of the counterterrorist era. The terms "Uzi" and "Tommy Gun" may have higher public profiles, but among special-operations units requiring weapons for "surgical" missions, the MP5 is very well known. It is known to many who watch films or television or play video games as well, since it is used as a visual shorthand for "the pros have arrived!" For decades it was the gun most closely associated with the black-clad operators against terrorists – in reality and on the screen.

DEVELOPMENT
A new kind of SMG

ORIGINS

SMG development after World War II

At the end of World War II, there were large numbers of SMGs in the armories of the victorious powers. Additionally, the early post-war years saw the development of the assault rifle/battle rifle, which precluded much of the need for the SMG. The Soviet Union and its satellites continued to use the PPSh-41 and PPS-43 SMGs, into the 1950s and 1960s, though the development of the SKS and AK-47 rifles eventually progressively led to their replacement. Nevertheless, the PPS-43 was produced until 1968 in the Soviet Union. In the hands of the North Koreans and the Chinese, the PPSh-41 and PPS-43 were widely used during the Korean War (1950–53).

In the British colonial counterinsurgency campaigns in Malaya and Borneo after World War II, the Sten and Sterling SMGs both saw wide use, as they were well suited for close combat in the jungle. SMGs also proved ideal for issue to British farmers in Kenya, as well as special counterinsurgency police units operating there between 1952 and 1960. For British armored crews, military police, and some specialist troops, the Sterling remained in service until at least the First Gulf War (1990–91). For decades, too, the suppressed Sterling remained the choice of many Western special-operations units for silent killing.

The United States ended World War II with the M3 "Grease Gun" as the primary SMG in use. It would continue to serve with some US special-operations units and armored crews until after the Vietnam conflict. In fact, when the Delta Force counterterrorist unit was originally formed in 1977, it was armed with the M3. Since US armed forces also had the handy, select-fire M2 Carbine available, there was little incentive to design

a new SMG. In the post-Vietnam era, therefore, instead of developing a new SMG for the US armed forces, US designers produced shorter-barreled versions of the M16 rifle, such as the Colt Commando. Within US law-enforcement agencies, the primary SMG in use remained the venerable Thompson. In fact, the FBI was still using the Thompson on a limited basis until the late 1980s. When the Los Angeles Police Department (LAPD) and other cities' law-enforcement agencies formed SWAT teams during the 1960s and 1970s, they were often armed with M16s rather than SMGs.

France, facing counterinsurgency wars in Indochina and Algeria, did develop a new SMG, the MAT 49, and it was good enough to remain in use for several decades. Influenced by the British Sten and American M3, the 9×19mm MAT 49 was developed as a quick and inexpensive weapon for arming French troops fighting overseas. Since French paratroopers were shouldering much of the burden in the counterinsurgency wars during the first decade after World War II, the MAT 49 was designed to meet their needs, with a wire telescoping stock and a magazine well that could be folded with magazine in place during a jump. Blowback operated, the MAT 49 fired from an open bolt at a cyclic rate of 600rds/min; since it did not have a semi-auto setting, the lower cyclic rate allowed better control in firing bursts. The MAT 49 remained in service with French military and police units from 1949 until 1979, when it was replaced by the 5.56×45mm FAMAS bullpup rifle. Employing stampings for ease of production, the MAT 49 was also chambered for the widely used 9×19mm caliber. It was extensively employed by both the French armed forces and the French police, especially the Gendarmerie Nationale. Also in 9×19mm caliber, the Beretta M12 was developed in 1959 in Italy and has continued in production. Easy to control owing to its front pistol grip, the M12 also employs a grip safety in addition to a manual safety. Though a well-designed SMG, the M12 did not enjoy large export sales.

The most influential SMG design of the early post-war years, though, was the Israeli Uzi. Developed in 1948 to give Israel a domestically produced weapon with which to arm its large army of citizen soldiers, the

Developed as a replacement for the Sten, the Sterling used a bolt with helical grooves, which aided reliability by removing dirt and fouling from inside the receiver as the weapon was fired. Also, unlike the Sten, which used a rudimentary safety notch into which the cocking handle was rotated, the Sterling had a selector switch. Another major improvement was in the magazine, which used a double roller system to align the cartridges much more uniformly than the Sten's magazine. The L2A1 Sterling was initially adopted in 1953, to be replaced by the L2A2 and L2A3 over the next few years; Sterlings remained in service with some British units into the 1990s. A suppressed version, the L34A1, was widely used by special-operations units until replaced by the MP5SD. Many L34A1s remain in armories today. (C&S)

9

Famed for its reliability and durability, the Israeli Uzi was the dominant SMG of the post-World War II era until the advent of the MP5, and remains in wide use today. Its compact open-bolt, blowback design made it a perfect weapon for special-operations/airborne units, armored crews, support troops, police, and Israeli workers needing a self-defense weapon. With more than 10,000,000 units sold, the Uzi can claim the title of most popular SMG of all time. Features such as the combination slider selector and grip safety make the Uzi a very safe weapon. Although the Uzi was initially designed as an open-bolt design, to compete with the HK MP5, closed-bolt versions of the Uzi have been produced as well. More compact versions such as the Mini-Uzi and Micro-Uzi have made it very popular with close-protection teams and others who need a clandestine SMG. (Author)

Uzi become the most popular SMG in the world for the next quarter-century. Employing a telescoping-bolt design that allowed the pistol grip to serve as the magazine well, thus allowing for a shorter weapon overall, the Uzi proved very popular when a concealable SMG was desired. Placing the magazine well in the pistol grip allowed faster, more instinctive reloads, based on the "hand finding hand" principle. The use of a grip safety also immediately rendered the SMG safe if the grip was relaxed. The Uzi was widely issued within the Israeli Army by the late 1950s, seeing extensive combat within the Arab–Israeli wars of the 1950s–1970s. By the 1960s it was also achieving wide export sales, which continued at least into the 1980s. Eventually, more than 90 countries would purchase Uzis for their military or police, and it would be produced on license by Belgium's FN Herstal. Among its most famous users were the US Secret Service, for protecting the US President. It was also produced under license in West Germany as the MP2 and used by the West German armed forces. The Uzi proved especially popular with combat-swimmer units, who found that it remained reliable even after it was submerged in water.

Although the HK MP5, the subject of this book, will be the best-known of the post-war German SMGs to most readers, two versions of the Walther MP – the MPK and MPL – were actually the more successful designs from the introduction of the MP in 1963 throughout the 1960s and into the early 1970s.

Towards the MP5

Always among the most prolific users of the SMG – beginning with the World War I MP 18/I and continuing with the World War II MP 38 and MP 40 – Germany resumed development of new SMG designs after World War II. The origins of the MP5 SMG can be traced to the development by Mauser of the Maschinenkarabiner Gerät 06 (Machine-Carbine Device

06; MKb Gerät 06), chambered for the 7.92×33mm *kurz* (short) round used in the Sturmgewehr 44 (Assault Rifle 44; StG 44) and other German assault rifle designs. This rifle employed a variation of the roller-locked short-recoil system used on the 7.92×57mm MG 42 general-purpose machine gun (GPMG) combined with a gas-actuated piston system. However, with experimentation Mauser engineers discovered that the gas system could be eliminated. The resultant roller-locked weapon was given the designation StG 45(M), but was not produced other than in prototype form. Generally accepted as the first assault rifle, the StG 44 influenced post-war development of the Soviet AK-47. Designed to take an intermediate cartridge, the StG 44's receiver was constructed of stamped and welded steel, resulting in a rifle that weighed 5.13kg when loaded. While the StG 44 used a gas system of operation, another German rifle – the StG 45(M) developed by Mauser – incorporated the roller-locking system that would later be used on the G3 rifle and MP5.

After the end of World War II, the French dismantled the Mauser plant and moved the machinery to France. Some of the engineers who had worked on the StG 45(M) went to work at the French Centre d'Études et d'Armement de Mulhouse (Mulhouse Armaments Study Center; CEAM) where two of the engineers, Ludwig Vorgrimler and Theodor Löffler, modified the StG 45(M) as the basis for a proposed new French rifle. Other prototype rifles were designed by Manufacture d'armes de Châtellerault (MAC) and Manufacture d'armes de Saint-Étienne (MAS). One of the weapons based on the StG 45(M), the Carabine Mitrailleuse Modèle 1950 (Machine-Carbine Model 1950), which had been designed by Löffler, performed well but owing to France's involvement in the First Indochina War (1946–54), it was deemed too expensive to adopt a new rifle.

Although the design had not been adopted in France, in 1950 Ludwig Vorgrimler moved to Spain to work for Centro de Estudios Técnicos de Materiales Especiales (Center for Technical Studies of Special Materials; CETME). Competing against former Rheinmetall engineers also working

The MPL. Even after the MP5 achieved substantial success, the MPK and MPL remained in production until 1985, being especially popular with the West German Bundespolizei. (T.J. Mullin)

Shown here in the semi-auto HK91 version and without its magazine, the G3 rifle ranks with the FN FAL as one of the most important post-World War II battle rifles. Developed initially by German engineers working in France, then Spain, after World War II, the G3 was developed by the Spanish firm of CETME but was eventually licensed for production in Germany by Heckler & Koch. The MP5 was considered a logical development from the G3 as it used the same roller-delayed blowback locking system. (National Firearms Museum)

at CETME, Vorgrimler, assisted by a team of former Mauser engineers, developed a prototype of their roller-delayed rifle chambered for the 7.92×40mm CETME cartridge. This rifle, designated the Modelo 2, was selected by the Spanish government to be developed further in July 1952.

Also interested in the Modelo 2 was the West German Bundesgrenzschutz (Federal Border Guard); however, this organization wanted a rifle in 7.62×51mm NATO caliber. Initially the Spanish thought the Germans wanted a 7.62mm version of the 7.92×40mm round. Eventually the misunderstanding was cleared up and the Modelo 2 in 7.62×51mm NATO caliber was produced as the Modelo B (the Modelo A fired a reduced-power 7.62×51mm round). In 1956, the Bundesgrenzschutz had adopted the Belgian Fusil Automatique Léger (Light Automatic Rifle; FAL) as the G1 battle rifle. In 1958, however, the Spanish government adopted the 7.62×51mm NATO CETME as the

Heckler & Koch

HK had been established at Oberndorf in 1949 by former Mauser employees Edmund Heckler (a former Mauser plant manager), Theodor Koch (a former Mauser engineer), and Alex Seidel (an industrial mechanic), but due to post-war restrictions the company could not produce weapons and instead manufactured bicycle parts, sewing-machine parts, and precision gauges. After these restrictions were lifted in 1954, however, HK became familiar with the CETME design since the firm had worked with CETME to allow that organization's weapon to fire the full-power 7.62×51mm NATO round. In 1969, HK became the sole producer of the G3 when Rheinmetall gave up their rights to produce the G3 in return for HK not bidding on a contract to produce the MG3 (Maschinegewehr 3, an updated version of the World War II-era MG 42). In 1977, the German government ceded HK complete sales and production rights to the G3.

British Aerospace acquired Royal Ordnance in 1987, followed in 1991 by the acquisition of Heckler & Koch GmbH (Gesellschaft mit beschränkter Haftung, which roughly translates as "limited liability company"). While part of British Aerospace, in 2000 HK received the contract to refurbish British Army SA80/L85 rifles, in the process fixing many of the deficiencies that had been found in the rifle during its service.

The resulting rifles, reportedly around 200,000, were designated L85A2. However, in 2002 BAE Systems, which included British Aerospace, restructured and HK was sold to a group of three German and one British investors who formed the German holding company HK Beteiligungs-GmbH. This holding company was restructured in 2003 to form a defense and law-enforcement group and a sporting-firearms group.

The MP5 was developed by HK in the 1960s to compete for the German police market, which required a substantial number of SMGs. Initially designated the HK54, the weapon entered development in 1964 as "Project 64." Designers who worked on the project included lead designer Tilo Moller and assistants Manfred Guhring, Georg Seidl, and Helmut Baureuter (James 2000: 65). As the project evolved, the weapon was given the designation HK54 using a numbering code employed by HK at the time. Under this code, the first digit for a light machine gun (LMG) would be "1"; a GPMG would have "2," a full-auto rifle "3," a semi-auto rifle "4," and an SMG "5." The second digit in the HK code referred to caliber, with "1" referring to 7.62×51mm NATO, "2" to 7.62×39mm, "3" to 5.56×45mm NATO, and "4" to 9×19mm (James 2000: 65). Under this system an HK SMG in 9mm would be the Model 54. Designations of weapons would often change when adopted for military service and marketed for civilian sales.

Variants of the MP5

HK54: The original version of what would become the MP5, produced by HK prior to 1966.

MP5A1: The first version of the MP5, with no stock and the "S–E–F" selector.

MP5A2: The version that would become the standard, with fixed stock and "S–E–F" selector.

MP5A3: With retractable stock and "S–E–F" selector.

MP5A4: With fixed stock and three-shot-burst trigger group.

MP5A5: With retractable stock and three-shot-burst trigger group.

MP5-SFA2: Single Fire (semi-auto) version with fixed stock.

MP5-SFA3: Single Fire (semi-auto) version with retractable stock.

MP5-N: US Navy model with "Navy" trigger group, retractable stock with rubber butt pad, and three-lug barrel threaded for a suppressor.

MP5F: Version for the French armed forces, featuring ambidextrous sling mounts, and beefed up internally to handle high-pressure ammunition.

MP5K: Compact version of the MP5, with or without folding stock, and "S–E–F" trigger group.

MP5KA1: Compact version with fixed rear sight and "S–E–F" trigger group.

MP5KA4: Compact version with the three-round-burst trigger group.

MP5KA5: As with the MP5KA1; fixed rear sight, but with the three-round-burst trigger group.

MP5K-N: US Navy version of the compact model with three-lug barrel threaded for suppressors and US Navy trigger group.

MP5K-PDW: "Personal Defense Weapon" (PDW) with characteristics of the MP5K-N but with a folding stock.

MP5SD1: Integrally suppressed version with no stock but instead an end cap, and "S–E–F" trigger group.

MP5SD2: Integrally suppressed version with fixed stock and "S–E–F" trigger group.

MP5SD3: Integrally suppressed version with retractable stock and "S–E–F" trigger group.

MP5SD4: Integrally suppressed version with no stock but instead an end cap, and three-round-burst trigger group.

MP5SD5: Integrally suppressed version with fixed stock and three-round-burst trigger group.

MP5SD6: Integrally suppressed version with retractable stock and three-shot-burst trigger group.

MP5SD-N1: Version with retractable stock, Navy trigger group, and fitted with a Knight's Armament Company (KAC) stainless-steel suppressor.

MP5SD-N2: Version with fixed stock, Navy trigger group, and fitted with a KAC stainless-steel suppressor.

MP5/10: Version in 10mm caliber in various stock and trigger-group configurations, principally for the FBI.

MP5/40: Version in .40 S&W caliber in various stock and trigger-group configurations.

HK94: A semi-auto version of the MP5 with 406.5mm barrel for US civilian sales.

SP89: A semi-auto version of the MP5K produced for US civilian markets without a stock so it qualified for sale as a pistol.

Modelo 58. The West German Bundeswehr (Federal Armed Forces), which had been formed in 1955, also acquired a number of the CETME Modelo B rifles for testing. In January 1959, the design was adopted by the West German government and licensed for production as the G3 by HK and Rheinmetall.

MP5 VARIANTS

The HK54/MP5

The HK54/MP5 used the HK roller-delayed bolt design for delayed-blowback operation. Among distinctive features of the HK54 not present on the later MP5 were a flip-up rear sight located over the magazine well,

13

An early MP5A2, showing the straight magazine, which was superseded in 1977 by a curved one to accommodate cartridges that would not feed reliably from the straight magazine. (Courtesy of HK USA)

cooling ribs on the barrel, two muzzle slots to act as a compensator, cooling slots cut into the forearm, and a longer and heavier bolt carrier. In 1966, it was adopted by West Germany's Bundesgrenzschutz, and some special units of the Bundeswehr.

The MP5A1, MP5A2, MP5A3, MP5A4, and MP5A5

When the MP5 designation was first applied to the HK SMG it referred to the fixed-stock model, while MP5A1 referred to the model with the retractable stock. Note that the MP5 is designed so that the stock options may be readily switched. Within a couple of years these designations would change.

On the MP5A2, the fixed-stock version of the HK SMG *c.* 1970, the selector switch has three options – "S" (*Sicher*, or "safe"), "E" (*Einzelfeuer*, or "single-fire" – semi-auto), or "F" (*Feuerstoss*, or "continuous fire" – full-auto). The "S" position is marked in white and the "E" and "F" positions in red. On some models of the MP5, including what is usually known as the "US Navy Model," selector positions are marked with red bullets in a rectangular box – a single one for semi-auto, seven in an open-ended box for full-auto, three in a closed box for burst, and single white

The trigger group from an MP5 manufactured by the Turkish firm Makina ve Kimya Endüstrisi Kurumu (Mechanical and Chemical Industry Corporation; MKEK), showing the "E–T–S" markings normally encountered on the Turkish versions, with "E" denoting safe, "T" semi, and "S" full-auto. Note that on HK-produced weapons using "red" or "white" bullet markings, the markings for the selector switch are in front of it rather than to the rear. It should be noted that some trainers of military special-operations units or police tactical units feel that the three-round or other "burst" trigger groups unnecessarily increase mechanical complexity, and therefore the chances of failure or – as has happened with units using burst trigger groups – improper assembly, leading to accidents. (C&S)

bullet in a white box with an "X" through it for safe. The fire-control or trigger group is contained within the pistol grip, which allows the mechanism to be switched out to allow other firing options (i.e. three-round bursts instead of full-auto).

The MP5SD

By the early 1970s the suppressed version of the MP5, the MP5SD (*Schalldämpfer*, or "sound dampener"), had been developed. It was available with a fixed stock, retractable stock, or butt cap for use without

An early MP5SD with the pre-1977 straight magazine. By the mid-1970s suppressed MP5s with the fixed stock were designated the MP5SD2 and those with the retractable stock the MP5SD3. With suppressed SMGs the most identifiable sound is often the bolt cycling back and forth, so in 1983 HK tested a locked-bolt version of the MP5SD, but this does not appear to have progressed past the prototype stage. (Courtesy of HK USA)

Manufacturing the MP5

Manufacture of the MP5 is designed for ease of production while still maintaining very high quality. The MP5's sheet-metal receiver is fabricated using 19 stamping operations. Grooves on each side of the receiver act as guides for the bolt carrier and also allow the buttstock group to be seated firmly. The hammer-forged barrel is press-fit to the receiver, then cross-pinned. Above the barrel, the tubular extension for the cocking lever and forward extension of the bolt carrier is welded to the receiver. A slot cut into the left side of this tubular extension allows the cocking handle to be pulled back or locked into the cocked position using the slot cut into the extension. The receiver and other external MP5 parts are phosphated then painted using an electrically charged painting technique. Earlier models have a more grayish appearance while later ones are matte black.

As with other HK weapons, the MP5 employs a fluted chamber, which allows gases to bleed rearward, thus preventing the case from expanding fully inside the chamber and thereby enhancing reliability. Prior to 1988, these flutes were the result of broaching the chamber, but after that date they were installed by the electrical discharge machining (EDM)

process. Broaching is a precision machining process in which a toothed tool, the broach, is pulled through the part to make the cut. In EDM, the cut is made by the discharge of electrical sparks. After the use of the EDM process to cut the flutes began, the number of flutes also increased from 12 to 16.

Over the decades it has been in service, there have been a significant number of modifications to the MP5. For example, in 1971, after the MP5 had been in service for five years, serrations were removed from the bolt group, the bolt carrier was shortened, trigger pull was lightened, and the ejection port was lengthened and a piece riveted to the port to improve ejection of spent cases. The next year, the chamber was altered slightly to improve feeding and synthetic keepers on the recoil-spring guide were added to impede battering of the buffer through recoil. Beginning in 1972 and extending into 1973, acrylic parts such as the trigger-group housing, forearm, and buttstock were strengthened with glass fiber. This addition substantially reduced the number of failures among acrylic parts. In 1973, the pistol grip was changed from a closed design to open, and the shape of the butt plate was changed from curved to flat. In 1975, a new cocking handle was introduced (James 2000: 72–80).

THE MP5 EXPOSED

9×19mm MP5A2

20
19
18
17
16
15
14
1
2
11 12 13
9
10
3
4
8
7
5
6

1. Cocking lever
2. Cocking lever support
3. Safety catch
4. Rotary rear aperture sight
5. Buttstock
6. Rear sling mount
7. Buttstock locking pin
8. Pistol grip
9. Trigger
10. Trigger guard
11. Magazine
12. Magazine follower
13. Cartridges in magazine
14. Cartridge in breech
15. Barrel extension
16. Barrel
17. Handguard
18. Handguard locking pin
19. Front sling mount
20. Lugs for barrel attachments
21. Guide ring
22. Bolt-head carrier
23. Firing-pin spring
24. Recoil spring
25. Ejector
26. Hammer spring
27. Ejector spring
28. Sear lock
29. Sear body
30. Trigger axle
31. Hammer
32. Hammer axle
33. Elbow spring/roller
34. Catch axle
35. Hammer anvil
36. Locking roller
37. Bolt head
38. Firing pin

A left-side view of an MP5SD3, with the paddle rather than button magazine release and the "S–E–F" trigger group. Although the MP5SD was designed for use with supersonic ammunition, it performs well with the 147-grain subsonic load originally developed for the US Navy SEALs and used by some US law-enforcement agencies. Frank James, noted firearms writer and submachine-gun specialist who has written extensively on the MP5, points out, however, that subsonic ammunition with a lower bullet weight will lose too much of its striking power due to the bleed-off of velocity (James 2000: 78). For best performance, it is normally recommended that supersonic 115-grain or 124-grain 9×19mm ammunition be used with the MP5SD. (C&S)

a stock, to aid concealment. The MP5SD's barrel is ported with 30 2.5mm holes and surrounded by a tubular casing, which contains helical baffles (diffusers). Escaping gases are diverted through the barrel's ports, allowing the helical baffles to reduce the sound level by increasing gas volume and decreasing temperature, thus dropping the bullet velocity by about 61m/sec to subsonic before it leaves the muzzle. In addition to the expansion chamber, the function of which has just been described, a second chamber diverts the gases as they leave the muzzle, muffling the report.

As the MP5 suppressor was a sealed unit that could not be disassembled for cleaning, it was normally recommended that fouling could be removed by detaching the suppressor, then pointing it upward and tapping its rear on a wooden surface, thus loosening and knocking out the fouling. If the

Although the MP5SD is the standard suppressed version, some units choose to use other suppressors; this MP5 mounts the Gemtech Raptor. Since 1993, HK USA – the US affiliate of Heckler & Koch GmbH, based in Columbus, Georgia – has offered the option of equipping an MP5 with the stainless-steel suppressor produced by Knight's Armament Company, first requested by US special-operations forces. Some operators link two magazines with various types of fasteners, metal or polymer; here black tape is used to link as well as to provide a better gripping surface. (Author)

Exterior features of the MP5

Muzzle:	End of barrel; location of the crown; threaded area on the Navy models		longer), butt cap, and folding varieties. The buttstock is the position of the rear sling mount
Three Lugs:	Locking lugs used to hold attachments	**Trigger Group:**	Held to the receiver with locking pins; contains the safety selector
Barrel:	Pressed and pinned into the barrel extension with standard land and groove configuration; free-floating	**Trigger Guard:**	Large for gloved hands
		Trigger:	Inside the trigger guard. Pulling it with the weapon loaded and off safe will fire the gun
Front Sight Holder:	Pressed, glued, and riveted to the barrel; holds the front sight and surrounds the cocking tube/cocking tube cap/front sling mount	**Safety Selector:**	Located on the trigger housing with multiple positions: Safe – Semi – 2-round burst – 3-round burst – Full-automatic. "Navy" selector is ambidextrous
Cocking Tube:	Welded to the front of the receiver; houses the cocking handle and mechanism and handguard locking pin bracket	**Magazine Well:**	Located in front of the trigger group, it accepts either 15- or 30-round magazines and holds the center sling mount (on 9mm variants)
Cocking Handle:	Used to pull the bolt group to the rear		
Receiver:	Formed and folded sheet metal; houses all assembly groups		
Scope Mount:	On each MP5, it provides a location and structure for a quick-detachable scope mount	**Magazine Release:**	Two position activation, button or paddle
		Ejection Port:	Located on the right side of the receiver; case deflector in port
Rear Sight:	Diopter in design, with four apertures for varying light conditions; adjustable with a tool for windage and elevation	**Handguard:**	Fiberglass or polymer; slim line or tropical; held in place by front locking pin [slimline handguards were the earlier type, which, as designated, were slimmer and easier to grip; these were replaced by the fatter "tropical" handguards] (HK International Training Division n.d.: 2–3)
Buttstock:	Held to the receiver with locking pin(s), buttstocks come in fixed, retractable (old-style metal back plate, new-style polymer plate, and Klausman style 1½		

carbon fouling is especially heavy it may be necessary to soak the suppressor in a non-oil based solvent. In this case it is important to check the O-ring, which helps prevent the suppressor from loosening, as the solvent may damage it and necessitate its replacement. HK also supplies a tool, which is used to clean the outside of the MP5SD's barrel and the ports when the suppressor has been removed.

The MP5K, MP5K-N, and MP5K-PDW

In 1976, the MP5K (*kurz*, or "short") was introduced, reportedly at the request of an HK sales representative in South America. Shorter and lighter to allow better concealment, the MP5K has a reduced-length barrel and barrel jacket, a very short bolt carrier, notches instead of apertures in the rotary rear sight to allow faster acquisition of the target, no stock initially but later – from 1991 – a folding stock, and a vertical foregrip to aid control in full-auto fire. On versions without the folding stock, the receiver's end cap has a ring for sling attachment. Skilled users learn to push the MP5K forward against the sling to gain some stability when firing.

An MP5K; note that this version has a butt cap with a sling swivel rather than a stock. Note also the vertical foregrip and the lip ahead of the foregrip to keep the hand from sliding forward in front of the muzzle. The standard barrel length for the MP5K is 114mm, but the MP5K-N developed for the US Navy SEALs has a 140mm threaded barrel. For comparison, the MP5A2 has a 226mm barrel. (C&S)

The shorter and lighter bolt carrier gives the MP5K a cyclic rate of approximately 100rds/min more than the standard MP5. The MP5KA1 has a fixed sight instead of the rotary-drum aperture sight. This version was often preferred for close-protection teams, as the more compact sight was less likely to snag when drawing the weapon from beneath a coat. For best concealment, a 15-round magazine was normally used with the MP5K.

The SMG II

A weapon with some similarities to the MP5K, designated the SMG II, was developed in 1984 by HK for a "classified" purchaser. Designed for compactness, the SMG II has a more ergonomic vertical foregrip, and the barrel is completely shrouded. Also, nothing protrudes from SMG II's butt cap; in contrast, on the MP5K a sling-swivel protrudes from the butt cap.

An MP5K-PDW of the type carried by aircrew of the US Army's 160th Special Operations Aviation Regiment (SOAR), which has the mission of inserting and extracting special-operations personnel behind enemy lines. Reportedly, one of the reasons the MP5K-PDW was developed was to arm this unit, which has a clear need for a conveniently carried weapon that still gives the crew substantial firepower if shot down. For the most part, however, SOAR crewmembers now carry M4 carbines. Here, the stock is deployed and the weapon lies on the thigh holster used by the unit. The green cord was used to tie the MP5K-PDW to the equipment so it did not get lost in a crash or during a quick exit from the aircraft. It also allowed the stock to be deployed simply by thrusting the weapon towards the target. (Jim Comparato)

The rear rotary sight is closer in type to that of the MP5 than the MP5K in that it incorporates "peep" apertures. Atop the SMG II receiver are two mounting brackets, which are different than those on other MP5s. These brackets are mounted far enough back that a cocking lever, which allows ambidextrous use as with the Uzi, is mounted atop the receiver. What appears to be the receiver cap of the SMG II is actually the buttplate of a sliding stock. Ambidextrous sling mounts are located on each side of the stock's base, and there are additional sling mounts on the front sight.

The SMG II actually has a lower receiver rather than the typical MP5 modules. This receiver contains the fire-control mechanism, the magazine well, magazine release, and bolt-lock button. The fire-control mechanism is of the "0, 1, 3, 30" type and uses an ambidextrous selector similar to those used on US Navy-model MP5s. The standard magazine is a polymer 30-round version. The ambidextrous magazine release is directly above the area in front of the elongated trigger guard. Another ambidextrous control, the bolt lock button mentioned above, is designed to lock the bolt closed so that there is no sound of the action cycling when using a suppressor. Also incorporated into the SMG II is a forward assist, such as that used on the M16/M4. Although this feature is useful to help chamber a round when the chamber is fouled, for the purpose of the SMG II it also allows a round to be chambered more quietly.

The SMG II's barrel is threaded for a suppressor, but the threads are about 89mm from the muzzle, allowing the "can" to slip over the muzzle. Ports in the barrel shroud, which contains the free-floating barrel, allow the operator to make sure the suppressor is mounted correctly (i.e. not canted). A gas valve controlled by a lever on the lower receiver allows gases to be bled off to reduce a standard velocity cartridge's bullet to subsonic velocity.

HK has never acknowledged for whom the SMG II was produced, nor the number built. However, most sources believe the number was somewhere in the 60–75 range. Some sources also attribute the SMG II contract to US special-operations forces such as the Combat Applications Group (Delta Force) and DevGru (SEAL Team Six). The SMG II seems to have had some influence on the development of the HK UMP, which will be discussed later.

Most likely for use with the SMG II, the US Navy reportedly at one point expressed interest in a 50-round drum for the MP5. However, the development around two decades ago of the Beta C-mag double drum magazine, which holds 100 rounds, made a 50-round drum far less desirable.

The MP5-N

The MP5-N was developed specifically for use by the US Navy SEALs and incorporates features specifically adapted to special operations. These include: an

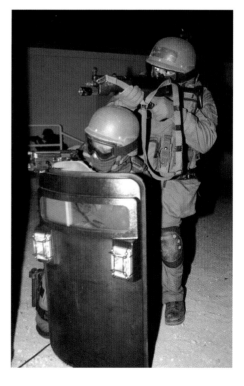

Members of a USMC SRT training for building-clearing operations. The "shield man" is armed with a pistol while his cover man is armed with an MP5. Personnel assigned to base SRTs and MARSOC (USMC Forces Special Operations Command) are the USMC's most common users of the MP5. (USMC)

ambidextrous three-position "Navy Trigger Group"; tritium front night sight; threaded barrel to take a Knight's Armament suppressor; and a retractable stock with rubber butt pad. The ambidextrous trigger group is an aid to firing from either shoulder, while the rubber butt pad helps retain the cheek weld when firing on full-auto. The SEALs find that suppressed weapons suit their clandestine mission, but also are well designed for Maritime Anti-Terrorism (MAT) missions on ships or oil platforms.

The MP5-SF

The MP5-SFA2, with "SF" standing for "Single-Fire," were fitted with a semi-automatic-only trigger group and were developed in 1986 to meet the FBI's requirement for a semi-auto 9mm carbine. There was also an MP5-SFA3 with a retractable buttstock. Law-enforcement agencies other than the FBI have purchased semi-auto versions of the MP5 for use as a patrol carbine. Armed British police units such as the Metropolitan Police's SCO19 (Specialist Crime and Operations) are also issued with semi-auto HK 9×19mm carbines.[1]

June 2010. A Metropolitan Police officer armed with an MP5-SFA3 on duty on Whitehall, Westminster, London. (© Mark Richardson / Alamy)

The MP5/10 and the MP5/40

Although the 9×19mm remains by far the most prevalent caliber in the MP5, the SMG has been chambered for other calibers. In the MP5/10, both the heavier and lighter variants of the 10×25mm auto cartridges may be used, and in the MP5/40, the .40 S&W (Smith & Wesson) round may be used. The 10mm round was developed to a large extent for the FBI, which adopted an S&W semi-automatic pistol, the Model 1076, chambered for the cartridge. Originally, the FBI used a heavy loading for the 10mm that provided ballistics superior to the .357 Magnum revolver cartridge. However, some agents had trouble handling the recoil of this round, so a lighter load was developed. To have an SMG in the same chambering as their pistols, the FBI experimented with converting one of their long-serving Thompson SMGs to 10mm caliber, but this experiment was not successful. As a result, the FBI approached HK about producing an MP5 chambered for the 10mm round, which resulted in the MP5/10.

The lighter 10mm load had ballistics similar to those of the .40 S&W load, which had been produced to meet requirements of the American law-enforcement market for a chambering more powerful than the 9×19mm round but less powerful than the .45 ACP. Within a few years, the .40 S&W round had become very popular with law-enforcement

---

1 For clarity it should be noted that SCO19 is the current designation for the unit. That name has changed over the years. Initially, the unit was known as D6, then as D11 in the early 1980s. That designation changed to PT17 in 1987, followed by SO19, then in 2012 BY SCO19.

Two versions of the MP5/10 developed for the FBI – at top is the A3 version and at bottom, the A2 version; note the straight polymer magazines, and that these versions have a two-shot-burst mode to allow fast double taps. (CSSA, Inc.)

agencies, and, in fact, the FBI stopped using their 10mm pistols and adopted the Glock 22 pistol in .40 S&W caliber. Both the MP5/10 and MP5/40 were introduced in 1992.

In addition to a different chambering, the MP5/10 and MP5/40 incorporated other changes. Unlike the standard 9×19mm MP5, they incorporated a bolt hold-open device with a bolt catch lever that could be operated to allow the bolt to travel forward after a reload. This combination allowed a faster reload in tactical situations. Incorporation of the hold-open device required the MP5's receiver to be altered to leave space for the mechanism. Additionally, the trigger-group housing had to be altered to allow installation of the bolt catch. The trigger group also required use of a different ejector for the 10mm- and .40 S&W-chambered weapons. The standard trigger group for the MP5/10 incorporated the three-round-burst mode, but according to *Jane's Infantry Weapons* the two-round-burst mode was developed specifically as an option for the MP5/10 allowing a fast "double tap" to the target. Also, presumably, the 10mm gun would generate greater recoil and muzzle rise on long bursts (Jones 2007: 113). On the MP5/10 and MP5/40, the muzzle came threaded for a suppressor. Instead of the magazine-release button on the right side of the magazine well used on the standard MP5, on the MP5/10 and MP5/40 a flapper magazine catch of the type used on many rifles is employed behind the magazine well. Tritium night sights were available for the MP5/10 and MP5/40.

On the MP5/10 and MP5/40 some parts (i.e. firing pin, firing pin spring, wire spring roller holder, and extractor spring) of the bolt group are the same as with the 9mm guns; however, major parts such as the bolt carrier, bolt head, recoil-spring guide-rod assembly, locking piece, extractor, locking rollers, and locking-roller holder (if from an older 9mm MP5) are not interchangeable. Because of the powerful heavy 10mm load, the MP5/10 uses the recoil spring from the 5.56×45mm NATO HK53. There are various other differences. The rollers in the bolt head are shorter on the 10mm and .40 S&W guns. This change was made so that the center of the bolt head was lowered enough to allow greater contact with the cartridge rims of the .40 S&W and 10mm rounds to enhance reliable feeding. Extractors and extractor springs are also different. The bolt carrier has an added protrusion to activate the hold-open device.

Since the two types of 10mm load vary greatly in the recoil impulse they generate, HK offered two different locking pieces for the bolt group. Locking pieces differ as the angles on their corners control the time and energy required to unlock the breech of the weapon after a round is fired.[2] For example, the angle for the MP5/40 "26" locking piece is 80 degrees, while the one for the "LO24" one is 90 degrees. The MP5/10 "HI25" for use with high-impulse (heavy recoiling) ammunition has a 60-degree angle. The locking piece for the lighter "low impulse" loads is marked "LO24," while the piece for the heavier loads is marked "HI25" (James 2000: 105). If the LO24 locking piece is installed in a weapon, the heavier loads may be used and will function reliably, but the battering may cause faster wear and may damage the recoil buffer. However, shooting low-impulse ammunition in a gun with the "HI25" locking piece may cause malfunctions. The HK Armorer's manual devotes four pages to use of LOW IMPULSE and HIGH IMPULSE 10mm ammunition and proper choice of the locking piece. Also included is a list of specific 10mm loads, giving their manufacturer, bullet weight and type, manufacturer's code, muzzle velocity, and the proper locking piece to be used. This detail was a good indication that care is needed when choosing the ammunition and locking piece combination for use with the MP5/10, and that experienced armorers were required.

Magazines for the MP5/10 and MP5/40 were made of translucent polymer to allow the operator to check quickly the number of rounds remaining. They were also designed so that they could be snapped together to allow a magazine to be inserted into the weapon while a ready spare rested alongside it. Initially, a stud-and-keyway system of locking the magazines together – much as with the Swiss Stgw 90 (SIG SG 550) – was

A right-side view of an MP5/40 with three-shot-burst mode and a SureFire forearm containing a weapon light. The MP5/40 was designed to offer various law-enforcement agencies an SMG chambered in the same caliber as their pistols. Among these agencies, the US DEA (Drug Enforcement Administration) showed early interest in the MP5/40. (C&S)

2   Markings on special locking pieces for other versions of the MP5 include: "5" or "SD" for the MP5SD; "16" for the MP5K; "80" for the PDW; and "26" or "LO24" for the MP5/40. Note that the "LO24" locking piece is used for the .40 S&W and also for the lower-powered 10mm round, as they are similar in recoil impulse.

A close-up of the MP5 bolt head showing the locking rollers, which are forced into recesses in the barrel extension to delay rearward movement of the bolt carrier after a shot is fired until the pressure generated by the cartridge has dropped. (C&S)

used, but instead a clamp was adopted. With practice by the user, this dual-magazine system made for a very fast reload. These magazines are straight and are 30 percent lighter than the standard 9mm magazines, a factor that helps compensate for the heavier 10mm or .40 S&W ammunition. They are also corrosion-resistant. Because the magazines are straight and have a greater circumference, alterations were required to the MP5 magazine well to accept them.

Reportedly, the FBI eventually ordered around 5,000 MP5/10s. HK produced spare parts for the MP5/10 to keep the FBI guns and any others sold operating, though the HK parts catalog does not currently show MP5/10 parts as available. It does, however, show parts available for the MP5/40 and the MP5/357. The latter was chambered for the .357 SIG round used by some US Federal agencies. Only the barrel and chamber of the MP5/357 would have to be different than the MP5/40, as the .357 SIG round uses a necked-down .40 S&W case. Although the Hostage Rescue Team (HRT) retains numbers of MP5/10s and others may be in FBI armories, some years ago 5.56mm AR-15 carbines replaced both 9mm and 10mm MP5s with the Bureau.

The MP5F/MP5E2

A noteworthy variation of the MP5 is the MP5F, which is usually identified as the version supplied for the French armed forces but was also designed to address some of the durability issues encountered in MP5s that had been in service for many years. Many MP5Fs were also purchased by US military and law-enforcement customers. The 1998 changes incorporated into the MP5F were the most substantial redesign of the MP5 in more than 25 years. The "F" in the MP5 designation is to signify "France," as the redesign was originally to meet requirements of the Gendarmerie Nationale. The official HK designation is MP5E2.

Many of the design changes arose from the desire of the Gendarmerie to use very "hot" 9×19mm ammunition ("hot" ammunition is loaded to a higher pressure and velocity than standard ammunition, and usually designated +P+). The MP5 had to be redesigned to meet the Gendarmerie tests, which would include firing 40,000 rounds through each of ten test weapons using the high-pressure 9mm ammunition. No parts failures were to be allowed and only a minimum of stoppages (Schatz 2000: 64).

The MP5F incorporated both internal and external changes. One of the most apparent is the incorporation of a 12.5mm-thick rubber butt pad. In addition to cushioning the weapon against the shoulder and inhibiting slippage against the shoulder when firing, this butt pad plus a slight lengthening of the stock increased overall length of the SMG by 17.5mm with stock folded. An increase of 25.4mm in the length of the stock forks allowed the forks to extend further into the stock, allowing more rigidity and less movement of the collapsible stock when firing. An additional sling-attachment point was added to the right side of the retractable stock. A second attachment was also added to the front sight base for right-hand attachment of a wider variety of tactical slings, including the ones used on the G36 and UMP (Schatz 2000: 65).

Internal changes are mostly to the bolt group. One MP5 part that had a reputation for failure after substantial use was the locking-roller holder. Primarily designed to keep the locking rollers in place in the bolt head when the MP5 is stripped, this holder is not actually necessary to fire the SMG, but it was beefed up for the MP5F. Also replaced was the firing-pin spring, a part that had been known to fail occasionally. For the MP5F this single-strand spring was replaced with a multi-strand spring, which provides longer service life and enhanced safety, since it gives greater resistance to an inertia strike of the firing pin on a primer if the weapon is dropped. A more durable extractor was developed as well (Schatz 2000: 67).

For the MP5F, the bolt-carrier assembly was changed to allow use of the heavier recoil-spring assembly developed for the MP5/10 and MP5/40.

An MP5A3 with the stock collapsed, a 1.5–6× scope mounted using the HK claw mount, and a 100-round Beta C-Mag in place. (Author)

The briefcase developed by HK to allow the MP5K to be carried concealed by undercover police officers or VIP protection teams, with the SMG mounted inside. Note that the muzzle fits into a port to allow it to be fired from within the briefcase, and that a trigger device inside the handle activates the SMG's trigger via a lever. (C&S)

Also from the MP5/10 and MP5/40, the shorter magazine-release lever is used, as it lowers the tendency to wear with a large number of magazine changes. To keep the cocking lever from unlocking from its forward position due to the heavier recoil generated by the French 9×19mm rounds, a two-part design used on the MP5/10 and MP5/40 was used in the MP5F (Schatz 2000: 67–68).

Virtually all of the improvements for the MP5F have now become standard in other models of the MP5. US government agencies that use 9×19mm +P+ loads have also adopted the MP5E2, in some cases actually before the French took delivery of their first guns. On the US MP5E2 weapons an additional feature is an extended selector switch.

ACCESSORIES

Mounts

In the early to mid-1970s, alterations to the MP5's receiver allowed the attachment of various mounts for optical sights, illuminators, or pointers. Among the options for mounting to the receiver were the HK claw mount often used on the HK G3. This mount employs a pair of spring-actuated bolts, affixed along the base of the mount and exerting pressure on the receiver. This system works well and assures that the mount allows the optics to hold their zero. Since it was initially designed for the 7.62×51mm G3, it holds up well to recoil. This quick detachable mount also is mounted high enough that the iron sights may be used through a "tunnel."

One of two optical sights was normally mounted – the Schmidt & Bender 4×25mm or the Hensoldt 4×24mm. The Zeiss 1.5–6× scope designed for use on the G3 is also sometimes encountered on the MP5. Night sights

One of the special cases used by German police to carry an MP5 in a Volkswagen T3, opened to show the SMG in place. Note that the case was actually designed for the older straight magazine rather than the later curved one shown. (C&S)

could be mounted, and underbarrel weapons lights or lasers may also be attached using the claw mount. More recently, instead of using the claw mount for a weapons light, many tactical law-enforcement or military special-operations users employ a SureFire forearm that incorporates a tactical light, which is operated by a pressure switch on the forearm.

Concealing the MP5

In 1978, a special briefcase was developed to carry the MP5K. A trigger concealed within the carry handle allows the case to be pointed at the target and the gun fired without its removal from the briefcase. Note that MP5Ks equipped with the ambidextrous selector may not be used in the briefcase. The briefcase system has proven quite popular with security teams protecting dignitaries. Shoulder-holster systems to carry the MP5K were designed for the same purpose.

TRAINING VARIANTS

As more military and law-enforcement agencies adopted the MP5, the demand for a training version grew commensurately. As a result, in 1970 a .22 Long Rifle (LR) conversion unit was introduced by HK. Consisting of a barrel insert, a bolt group with recoil springs, and two 20-round

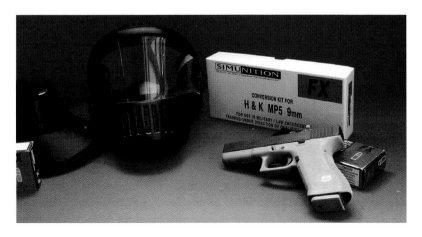

A Simunition Kit for the MP5 along with a "Blue Glock" used to fire Simunition rounds, some Simunition marking cartridges, and the face and neck protection worn when training with Simunition. (T.J. Mullin)

magazines, the conversion unit was designed to allow low-cost training on indoor ranges. The .22 conversion units did not prove reliable, however, and fewer than 400 were produced. A much more effective training version of the MP5 is the MP5T ("T" for training), developed in 1984 for use with Dynamit Nobel plastic training ammunition. Marked "only plastic training" on each side of the receiver in blue text and with a blue cocking lever, the MP5T is not intended for use with live ammunition, as this model has no locking rollers in its bolt head. Care must be still taken when using the MP5T, as the bullets have a velocity of approximately 213m/sec and can travel to 170m. The "T" model uses a floating chamber so that recoil approximates that of a full-power 9×19mm load.

Instead of the MP5T, many agencies that use the MP5 now use the Simunition conversion kit, which allows standard versions of the MP5 to fire dye-marking training ammunition for force-on-force training, though trainees must still wear masks and protective clothing when using Simunition weapons. Simunition are popular enough for use with the MP5 that conversion units are now made for the MP5, MP5SD, and MP5K.

Also useful for training purposes is the "Red Gun" version of the MP5 produced by Armament Systems and Procedures (ASP), best known for producing the ASP baton used by police all over the world. The same size and configuration as the MP5A2, the polymer training weapon is useful for an array of tactical training where live fire is not required or advisable. For example, when practicing assaults on buildings, buses, aircraft, ships, etc., the red MP5 may be carried and used while conducting the operational maneuvering and teamwork. ASP also makes a red polymer training magazine for use with the MP5.

A red polymer MP5 produced by ASP for training in tactics and retention. Once basic techniques and movements have been mastered, operators can move on to "Blue" Simunition guns, and eventually – if live-fire tactical ranges are available – to live-fire drills. (Author)

CIVILIAN VERSIONS

Since the standard MP5, with a very few exceptions imported early into the United States, was not normally legal for civilian sales, two semi-automatic versions were developed for the US civilian market. The HK94 was a semi-automatic carbine version with a 420mm barrel. Many purchasers did not like the look of the HK94 due to its overly long barrel, but there were a couple of "fixes." A fake suppressor could be added that made the HK94 appear to be an MP5SD, or the carbine could be licensed with the Bureau of Alcohol, Tobacco, Firearms, and Explosives (BATFE) as a short-barreled rifle (SBR) and the barrel cut to the standard SMG length. HK94s are actually quite scarce in the United States, as many have been purchased for modification into an "MP5" select-fire weapon using a registered sear. Due to the intricacies of US Federal firearms laws, if properly registered such weapons are legal; the MP5 used for the shooting tests in this book is such an altered "sear" gun.

The second version of the MP5 designed for civilian sales in the United States is the SP89, which is a semi-automatic pistol that resembles the MP5K. To meet requirements for sale as a pistol, the SP89 does not allow the attachment of a shoulder stock and does not have the vertical foregrip, though it does have a slight protrusion that extends down from the forearm so that the hand does not slip in front of the muzzle when firing the weapon. The SP89 was only imported for five years, and, like the HK94, is popular for conversions. It may be registered as an SBR and converted to a semi-auto that resembles an MP5K or it may be converted to an SMG using a registered sear as discussed above.

The HK VP70

In addition to the MP5, HK also produced a machine pistol – the VP70 – for almost 20 years from 1970. "VP" stands for *Vollautomatische Pistole*, which translates as "Fully Automatic Pistol." In many ways, the VP70 was quite innovative, since it used a polymer frame a decade before the introduction of the similarly structured Glock pistol in 1982. It had an 18-round magazine capacity, quite high for the time. Also, like some

The VP70 was produced from 1970 until 1989 and achieved a few military or law-enforcement sales to countries such as Morocco, Paraguay, and Portugal. Since the stock/holster was somewhat cumbersome, most users preferred to purchase an SMG such as an MP5, or if compactness was paramount, the MP5K. A reasonable number of VP70Z semi-auto-only versions were sold in the USA, but it never really achieved the popularity of later HK pistols.

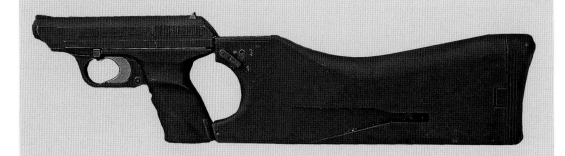

current pistols, it was a double-action-only design, meaning that it was necessary to use the longer double-action pull for each round, while other pistols of its time required a double-action pull for the first round but lighter single-action pulls for subsequent rounds, since the action of the slide would cock the hammer. Even though it is double-action only, the VP70 still incorporates a cross-bolt safety.

ABOVE One feature of the VP70 is the use of a pistol stock/holster, which actually incorporates the selector switch. Without the stock affixed, the VP70 can only function as a semi-automatic pistol. Note the selector switch for single rounds or three-shot-burst. Once the stock is affixed, the pistol can be fired in three-round-burst mode. The attachment point for the stock is somewhat fragile and with a lot of use may break. (Author)

USE
Full-auto accuracy in action

OPERATION

Unlike most other SMGs of the 1960s, the MP5 fires from a closed bolt, which enhances accuracy. Simply put, this means that unlike open-bolt SMGs, in which the bolt moves forward when the trigger is pulled, in a closed-bolt design only the hammer moves forward to strike the firing pin. Open-bolt guns are fired when the heavy bolt goes forward and the firing pin strikes the cartridge primer as the bolt closes. This movement, the abruptness of the bolt hitting the chamber face, and the immediate firing of the cartridge make it very difficult to retain the sight picture when the

Members of the Singapore Coast Guard and a US Marine Fleet Antiterrorism Security Team (FAST) train together on boarding and ship-clearing operations during August 2011. Note that the MP5 in the foreground mounts a blank-firing device. Both MP5s are taped with blue tape, which is normally used to indicate that they have been checked to ensure no live rounds are loaded in the weapon or magazine. (USMC)

HK MP5 operating sequence

The MP5 will normally be carried slung across the chest or in the hands in the "low ready" position. If the fixed-stock MP5A2 is used, it is ready for action immediately. If the MP5A3 version is used, normally the stock will have been extended unless it is being carried in a vehicle or in other situations where space is limited. To extend the stock, the lever located behind the receiver is pressed while the stock is pulled rearward (**1** and **2**). Also to prepare the MP5 for action a magazine will be inserted and tapped on the baseplate to make sure it is fully seated (**3**). Note that if the MP5 is to be carried with the bolt forward and chamber empty on a loaded magazine, only 29 rounds may be loaded in a 30-round magazine or the magazine will not seat in the magazine well.

Normally, unless immediate action is anticipated, the MP5 will be carried with the loaded magazine in place, but the chamber empty. The user must determine where he wants the selector switch in this

weapon is fired on full-auto. With the closed-bolt MP5, it is far easier to hold the sight picture. One "disadvantage" sometimes cited for closed-bolt full-automatic weapons is what is known as "cook-off," which can cause a spontaneous discharge of the weapon. Normally, cook-off can occur when the temperature in the weapon's chamber exceeds 250 degrees Celsius (482 degrees Fahrenheit) for more than a minute with a round in the chamber. However, experts have determined that the temperature of the 9×19mm round does not produce even close to 250 degrees Celsius and even MP5s fired continuously in training or testing have not experienced cook-off.

When closed, the MP5 bolt engages the barrel extension, which is welded to the receiver. As with the G3 rifle, the bolt consists of two parts – a bolt head with rollers and the bolt carrier. When a round is chambered and ready to fire, the bolt carrier rests against the bolt head. To prevent bolt rebound as the bolt goes forward, the carrier contains loose tungsten granules under the recoil-spring barrel/tube. These granules help to delay the arrival time of the carrier mass at the forward extent of its travel, thus damping the impact of the bolt by spreading the mass among various parts when it returns to its forward position. Slanted planes at the front

situation. He may leave it on safe, place it on single-shot, or place it on full-auto. If on safe, when he chambers the first round he will also have to flip the safety to one of the fire positions. With practice, an operator can do both simultaneously (**4**). Some operators choose to have the chamber empty but the selector set on single-shot or full-auto ready to fire as soon as the bolt is operated. When the MP5 is carried with a round chambered, normally the selector is carried on safe.

Once a round is in the chamber and the selector is set on one of the fire positions, the operator will acquire his sights (**5**). When targets are engaged, the operator will normally fire a short burst or two or three rounds into each enemy, either through trigger control or by utilizing the three-shot-burst setting, if available (**6** and **7**). When the magazine is empty, on most MP5s (the .40 S&W and 10mm versions have bolt hold-open devices) the bolt does not lock back so the operator will have to release the empty magazine (**8**) and repeat the loading procedure.

of the locking piece force the rollers into recesses in the barrel extension to "lock" the bolt. When the round is fired, expanding gases are transmitted to the bolt head as the spent case leaves the chamber, which transmits some of the force to the rollers that project from the bolt head. These rollers cam inwards against the slanted portions of the locking recesses in the barrel extension and the angled shoulders of the locking piece.

After the bolt carrier, which travels rearward at four times the velocity of the bolt head, has moved 4mm, the locking piece is fully retracted from the bolt head (which has moved only 1mm), allowing the rollers to compress into the bolt head. It should be noted that some authorities emphasize that the rollers do not really lock the bolt, but instead exert a "retarding effect" upon it (Nelson & Musgrave 1980: 409). In any case, this process creates enough of a delay that gas pressure has dropped to a safe level before the case leaves the chamber and the bolt opens. The heavy bolt carrier also exerts at least some slowing of the bolt's rearward progress. Once the bolt reaches the extent of its rearward travel and the empty case has been extracted, the return spring compresses and forces the bolt forward to chamber a round and force the rollers outward to relock the bolt.

The MP5's rear sight is a diopter drum offering four apertures to allow greater or lesser light to suit the shooter. Note that the different apertures are not for varying distances, but are designed to offer more precision or faster target acquisition. On the early HK54 models, a flip-up rear sight was positioned rather far forward above the magazine well. By 1966, however, the rotary drum rear sight was being used. Tritium inserts are available for both front and rear MP5 sights. (C&S)

Jane's Infantry Weapons 2007–2008 offers a more detailed technical description of the MP5's operations:

… a two-part bolt with rollers projecting from the bolt head. The more massive bolt body lies up against the bolt head when the weapon is ready to fire. Inclined planes on the front lie between the rollers and force them out into recesses in the barrel extension. The gas pressure places backward force on the bolt head, which is unable to go back, since the rollers are in the recesses in the barrel extension and must move in against the inclined planes of the heavy bolt body. The selected angles of the recesses and the incline on the bolt body produce a velocity ratio of about 4:1 between the bolt body and the bolt head. Thus, the bolt head moves back only about 1mm, while the bolt body moves some 4mm. As soon as the rollers are fully in, the two parts of the breech are driven back together. The empty case is held to the breech face by the extractor until it strikes the ejector and is thrown out of the ejection port on the right of the gun. The return spring is compressed during the backward movement of the bolt and drives the bolt forward. A round is fed into the chamber, and the bolt face comes to rest. The bolt body continues to move forward, and the inclined planes drive the rollers into the barrel extension recesses. The bolt body closes up on the bolt head, and the weapon is ready to fire another round. (Jones 2007: 112)

A US Tier One operator fires the MP5/10. He leans well into the weapon when firing full-auto (note the selector is on full); a solid shooting stance is even more important in firing the heavier-recoiling 10mm-caliber weapon. The MP5/10 was known for superior accuracy and, using the heavier loads, for excellent penetration. Although HK discontinued the MP5/10 due to lack of purchasers, the FBI was happy with the weapon and members of its Hostage Rescue Team (HRT) as well as regional FBI SWAT teams continued using it for some years. (CSSA, Inc.)

The MP5's free-floating, cold-hammer-forged barrel is an aid to accuracy as well. In simple terms, a free-floating barrel does not touch the stock at various points, thus preventing contact with the stock affecting barrel harmonics and accuracy.

Prior to 1977, the MP5 used a straight double-column box magazine, but after that date the magazine was given a slight curve. Reportedly, this was to enhance reliability with some special types of ammunition, especially the Dynamit Nobel BAT (Blitz Action Trauma) round. Note that a Beta C-Mag (Century magazine, holding 100 rounds) is also available for the MP5.

Owing to the MP5's modular construction it is easy to re-configure it by changing the buttstock or trigger group. The six assembly groups are: barrel/receiver group; bolt group; trigger group; buttstock; forearm; and magazine. The most common assembly groups that are changed are the trigger group and the buttstock. Magazines with different capacities may be used as well.

The MP5's cocking handle is located above the hand guard towards the front of the SMG. It does not reciprocate during firing. This cocking handle is attached to a tubular device known as the cocking-lever support. The cocking-lever support contacts with the forward portion of the bolt group when being pulled rearward to cock the bolt. The cocking handle may be locked to the rear by rotating it into a slot in the cocking-lever tube.

It is normally possible to tell when an MP5 or another 9×19mm HK weapon has been fired on a range as the spent brass displays marks from the weapon's fluted chamber. These flutes (essentially longitudinal grooves

in the surface of the chamber) enhance reliability since gas bleeding back through them helps prevent cases from sticking in the chamber as they expand. Flutes are also very important for the MP5 as the roller-delayed action leads to violent extraction. Without these flutes to allow gas to "float" the fired case out of the chamber, the extractor would rip through the case rim.

A close-up of the three muzzle lugs on the MP5, which allow various devices, including a flash suppressor, blank-firing device, and two types of grenade launchers – one for rifle-type grenades and one for gas grenades – to be quickly fitted or removed. (C&S)

The MP5's cocking handle locks open by rotating it into the slot in the cocking lever tube. As the standard MP5 does not have a bolt hold-open device, this is the only method for locking the bolt in the rearward position. Experienced users learn to slap the lever with the support hand to run it forward quickly. Interestingly enough, one of the best portrayals of this technique is by Dame Helen Mirren in the 2010 film *RED*. (C&S)

THE MP5 IN LAW-ENFORCEMENT SERVICE

GSG 9

At least indirectly, the rising profile of the HK MP5 can be attributed to the tragic massacre of Israeli athletes at the 1972 Munich Olympics. The German police who unsuccessfully tried to rescue the Israelis from the Olympic Village were armed with SMGs, but they were Walther MPLs. However, since the attempt was aborted due to the terrorists seeing their approach on television, the MPLs did not play a part in the crisis. However, as a result of the terrorist action, the West German government formed a counterterrorist unit, specifically trained to deal with future terrorist incidents. Less than a year after the death of the Israeli athletes, on April 17, 1973, GSG 9 was established as part of the Bundesgrenzschutz. One of the standard weapons of the Bundesgrenzschutz was the MP5; hence, it was a primary weapon for GSG 9.

GSG 9 operators used the MP5A2 as their standard weapon, but also had the MP5SD and the MP5K, the latter for special missions requiring greater concealment. GSG 9 developed an array of tactics using the MP5, including firing from helicopters at vehicles or terrorists. The unit also had vehicles with special gun ports built into the windshields, so that the occupants could engage vehicles with their MP5s during pursuits. Although

GSG 9 operators during the early days of the unit (the year indicated by the straight magazines in their MP5s) training in assault techniques. With GSG 9 and later counterterrorist units, the MP5 proved especially well suited for hostage-rescue missions. It was compact, which allowed operators to move through confined spaces quickly. It was accurate and ergonomically friendly and allowed multiple shots to be placed on a terrorist quickly. The 9×19mm cartridge was not as likely as a rifle round to over-penetrate during rescues aboard aircraft, ships, or in apartment blocks or other buildings. Recoil was also light enough with the 9×19mm round that operators quickly learned to fire controlled bursts into the head or torso of a "Tango" or "X-Ray," as various counterterrorist units designated their terrorist targets. (Author's collection)

GSG 9 had available optical sights and illuminators for use in low-light conditions, they used their MP5s with the standard sights much of the time.

GSG 9 became world famous on October 17, 1977, when the unit carried out a rescue of passengers aboard a Lufthansa aircraft that had been hijacked to Mogadishu, Somalia. The rescue, codenamed "Fire Magic," was launched at 0200hrs local time; within five minutes the operators had secured the aircraft, neutralized the terrorists, and freed all of the hostages. Principal armament of the assault team had been handguns and the MP5. Handguns had been chosen to allow the operators to get through doorways more quickly, but they did not incapacitate some of the terrorists instantly. The MP5s, by contrast, performed admirably, stopping terrorists instantly with bursts. This operational experience would influence GSG 9 to rely more heavily upon the MP5 during future operations. SAS observers, who supplied GSG 9 with stun grenades, were

A close-up of the MP5's front sight. A front post is protected by a hooded ring, which also helps in quickly aligning the sights. MP5 sights are also better than those of most other SMGs. Generally, the MP5 leaves the factory with the sights set for 25m. (Author)

present. Since the SAS had also adopted the MP5 at this point, they were pleased to see that the weapons performed well. Barry Davies, one of the SAS men present, describes the GSG 9 actions in his book *Fire Magic*:

> The assault teams put on their British-made body armor and fitted up their Heckler & Koch MP5 machine guns in the same way as the SAS. However, it would appear that most of the first wave going into the aircraft would be using pistols. This may seem a little strange, but they first had to get through a small hatch where a larger weapon would be cumbersome, and in a confined space like an aircraft a pistol is more flexible. Not that I liked the Germans' choice of handguns – they were using either small 9mm P9s[3] or the Smith & Wesson .38 Special Revolver. Give me the Browning Hi-Power every time – not only does it give you thirteen shots, but it tends to stop whatever you hit. (Davies 1994: 138–39)

However, according to Davies, the first terrorist kill was carried out by an MP5 as a GSG 9 operator on an assault ladder fired a burst into a female terrorist just inside one of the aircraft's doors, killing her instantly (Davies 1994: 142). Although the MP5 in various configurations is still an important GSG 9 weapon today, currently they also use other weapons for assaults including the HK 416 and HK 417 carbines, G36/G36K/G36C, and HK MP7A1.

The FBI

When the FBI formed their HRT in 1982 they did a lot of their initial training with Delta Force, the SAS, and other Tier One[4] counterterrorist units. As a result, they also adopted the MP5 SMG. Danny Coulson, the founder of the FBI HRT, has commented on how the operators learned to value the MP5 as they carried out hostage-rescue drills with Delta Force:

> These drills really made us appreciate our new weapon – the Heckler and Koch MP5 submachine gun. It was the weapon of choice for Delta, the SAS, and other European counterterror teams, but most of the HRT trainees had never wielded one before they came to the team. Once they did, they fell in love. The MP5 was extremely accurate. At twenty-five yards, you make group[5] in a target no bigger than a half dollar. It was easy to operate and completely reliable. Cold, rain, snow, mud, sleet – the MP5 did its job. It was compact with a telescoping stock so it could be fired like a conventional shoulder weapon or, with the stock collapsed, used for close-quarter combat. (Coulson & Shannon 1999: 171)

---

3   Davies may mean that GSG 9 was using the HK P7 pistol when he says they had "P9s," as the P7 was the standard GSG 9 semi-automatic pistol at the time.
4   "Tier One Units" is a term designating the most elite of elite units, such as the SAS, SBS, SEAL Team Six (DevGru), Delta Force (CAG), etc.
5   "Group" refers to the measurement between the center of the holes punched by three shots or five shots to determine accuracy. "Group" is the term used with respect to rifles, SMGs, or pistols, while "pattern" refers to shotguns.

From Coulson's description it seems the HRT was using MP5A3 models. However, Coulson also indicates that they had MP5SDs for special missions. He describes a reconnaissance around a compound in Arkansas occupied by members of an anti-government group:

> We checked our maps, verified our position, and started our patrol. We traveled light. Core carried his Heckler & Koch MP5 suppressed submachine gun with an aim point projector for accurate nighttime firing. Bonney, Warford, and I packed our Browning Hi-Powers. Wiley took his Colt Car-15. Buford also took a semi-automatic pistol. Every man had two flash-bangs, a handy-talky, two spare batteries, and night-vision equipment. Most of the men used PVS-5 night-vision binoculars. I preferred a PVS-4 monocular because I could reconnoiter with one eye using the infrared or light intensive capability of the device, while keeping the other eye free. (Coulson & Shannon 1999: 235)

It is interesting to note that the members of the HRT on this specific operation felt that a mix of weapons such as a suppressed MP5SD for dealing with members of the group at close range silently during an approach might be valuable, but also believed that the greater stopping power and penetration of the 5.56×45mm CAR-15 might be required.

GIS

Another highly trained counterterrorist unit that has made good use of the MP5 is Italy's Gruppo di Intervento Speciale (Special Intervention Group; GIS) of the Carabinieri.[6] GIS became operational in 1978 and has been assigned an array of counterterrorist and counter-Mafia operations over the subsequent years. Although GIS initially used Beretta's 9×19mm PM-12 SMG, the organization soon switched to the MP5 after encountering it in use with other elite units with which they trained. GIS operators primarily use the MP5A5, MP5SD3, and MP5KA4, the latter mainly for VIP protection assignments. Since GIS uses the Firearms Training System (FATS), which projects live-action scenarios on screen to which operators react using a laser-equipped weapon, it may be presumed that they have MP5s set up for FATS.

This GIS operator, in position atop an assault vehicle, assumes a cover position with his HK MP5A5. It incorporates a SureFire forearm with weapon light; a laser pointer is mounted on the receiver. (Author's collection)

6   Although the Carabinieri is one of Italy's four armed forces, its use of the MP5 is discussed here under law enforcement as that is the Carabinieri's primary role, rather than under military use.

The NSG

India's National Security Guard (NSG), which was formed in 1986 and given an array of counterterrorist duties, uses the MP5 as its principal building-assault/hostage-rescue weapon. In response to the November 26–29, 2008, terrorist attacks in Mumbai, India, members of the NSG were deployed. Among the targets were two hotels: the Taj Mahal Hotel and the Oberoi Trident. At about 7am on the morning of November 29, members of the NSG used an explosive device to blow the remaining terrorist from behind a large pillar behind which he was hiding. He was literally blown out of the hotel; to make sure he was dead, an NSG sniper put a bullet in his head (Scott-Clark & Levy 2013: 271–72). All of the remaining terrorists, except for one captured, had already been killed. During the attack at the two hotels and two other venues, a total of 166 civilians and security personnel were killed, along with nine of the ten terrorists. The terrorist who was captured was interrogated and supplied Indian police and intelligence personnel with information about the planning of the operation. During operations at the various sites seized by the terrorists, the NSG, with assistance from India's MARCOS Naval Commandos, had to clear 900 rooms, during which they reportedly killed eight terrorists (NSG sources state they killed eight terrorists, though other sources state a total of nine were killed) and rescued more than 600 hostages. The captured terrorist was later executed by hanging.

The NSG has an array of MP5 variants in its armories, including the MP5A3, MP5A5, MP5SD3, MP5SD6, MP5K, and MP5K-PDW. About two-thirds of the MP5s in a 2009 NSG order from HK were MP5A3s, but there have been delays in the deliveries; it may be presumed that it will be the most commonly encountered model at the time of writing. The latter two "K" models would normally be used when assigned to VIP protection

duties or when it is necessary to hide the weapon on clandestine entries. In the years since the Mumbai terrorist attack, weapons and equipment of the NSG have been upgraded, including laser designators for the MP5s.

The NSG operator at left helps his commander adjust the sling of his MP5; these members of the NSG are part of the regional detachment stationed in Mumbai after the November 2008 terrorist attacks. (AFP/Getty Images)

SCO19

Among the best-known police users of the MP5 in the United Kingdom are the members of the Metropolitan Police's ARVs. There have been indications that some armed units of the Met may be currently using the rifle-caliber G36 to give them the ability to deal with criminals or terrorists armed with rifles. Over the years between 1966, when the forerunner of the later units was formed, and the time of writing the Specialist Firearms Command has had various designations. The designation at the time of writing is SCO19. Primary weapons for the unit are the Glock 17 pistol – also in 9×19mm caliber – and the "Single Fire" (semi-automatic) HK MP5. ARV officers as well as police assigned to London airports use the MP5 as an urban carbine, which allows the officer to engage more effectively at ranges of 45m or more, yet will not offer the range nor the penetration of a rifle (the latter being a disadvantage in an urban area). The choice of a semi-automatic version also fits most missions of armed British police.

The MP5 carbine has been in service since July 1991, as long as the "Met" have been deploying ARVs – the Trojan Cars. Initially, the handgun issued was the six-shot S&W Model 10 .38 Special revolver, so the higher magazine capacity and greater range of the MP5 was a definite advantage. In *The Trojan Files*, Roger Gray, who was assigned to ARVs when the unit was formed in 1991, has some interesting comments about the MP5. He recalls his introduction to the weapon:

The next day dawned bright, and the prospects of the coming hours were discussed. This was to be an introduction to our "primary weapon." The Gurkha has his knife and the ARV man has his MP5. For me it was to become a working relationship: good to have the gun around but we never really got on.

The three days that followed were purgatory. Magazine in ... make ready ... selector lever to fire ... stoppage ... selector lever to safe. I had that one all the time. What's this bloody stoppage lark? Revolvers don't "stop." (Gray 2000: 53)

Gray goes on to recount his training with the MP5, as he learned to shoot it from various positions and practiced malfunction drills constantly. He then goes on to describe why it was a good choice for the ARVs:

Actually, it's a damned good weapon. Derived from a machine gun. The Metropolitan Police version as carried by ARV crews fires single shots of nine-millimetre, soft-pointed ammunition in common with the Glock self-loading pistol. These rounds are designed to spend all their energy within the selected target, creating maximum knock-down but, more importantly, to avoid overpenetration. Put simply, they're designed not to pass through and strike a second person.

Its accuracy is like a surgeon's knife compared with the mallet that a handgun can be. Within the confines of a suburban environment, that accuracy could actually save innocent lives, placing the rounds precisely where they were intended. (Gray 2000: 53)

In their concern that ARV officers might react precipitously in deploying their weapons, Metropolitan Police policy for deploying and using the weapons was quite strict. It included keeping the MP5 carbines carried in an ARV in a secure vault in the vehicle, which sometimes required some effort to open and retrieve the weapons. Gray describes one ARV run to deal with a man armed with a rifle:

Darren had slipped into the garden of the adjoining house and, using the high conifers as cover, he peered over the low brick wall. The man in the camouflage gear and beret was looking directly at him. In his belt was the huge sword, in his hands a Lee-Enfield .303 rifle. He raised it, aimed at Darren, and fired.

The shout of "Armed Police" came instinctively from his lips, as Darren then pulled the trigger of the .38. He got two shots off as the gunman ducked back in the doorway, the sound of the rifle bolt going forwards clearly audible. Darren backtracked out to the street.

Sandy was trying to extract the carbines from the safe concealed behind the centre armrest of the rear seat. The gunman suddenly appeared at the gate, aimed at her and fired. He hit the windscreen and pillar of the car. On the side of her head the blood had begun to flow but adrenaline killed the pain. She must get the carbines. (Gray 2000: 99)

The female officer was hit by shotgun pellets fired by the suspect – possibly from a converted .303 rifle – but the two other officers from the vehicle returned fire with their S&W revolvers. Though wounded, she managed to pass an MP5 carbine to one of the other officers. The subject had retreated into a house but came back out and was shot and arrested. The female officer was treated for her injuries (Smith 2013: 110).

The situation described was one that could have seen the outgunned ARV team killed or seriously injured had the shooter been more aggressive. It is important that police long guns should be transported securely, but also be ready for quick deployment when a threat is encountered. In many US police patrol cars, the longarms are carried in a rack on the roof of the vehicle or on the floor. Although the racks may have key locks, they often also have an electronic quick-release lock operated by a concealed button. However, the ARV teams learned to live with what they had and displayed courage, in some cases deploying an officer with a handgun to cover the officer extracting the carbines from the transport safe.

Even though the ARV personnel dealt with armed and dangerous criminals, and trained constantly with their weapons, they were actually involved in few shooting incidents. In *Urban Warrior*, written by one of the first women in the ARVs, Helen Barnett points out that in 1997, of 1,765 operational deployments, SO19 (designation changed to CO19 in 2005 and SCO19 in 2012) officers fired shots only once (Barnett 1999: 205). Steve Collins – who joined after 1987, when the designation was changed to PT17 – recalled his first experience with the MP5 in the book *The Good Guys Wear Black*:

"The Heckler & Koch MP5 A2 Carbine." The instructor spoke in a high-pitched voice that had years ago earned him the nickname Squeaky.

Hoisting the sinister-looking short-barrelled weapon aloft, he continued. "Now standard issue to Level One and Level Two Teams. When you take this out consider it your primary weapon; the Glock will be carried as a backup."

... Squeaky continued: "Made by Heckler and Koch in Oberndorf, Germany, since the 1960s, and carried by most major counterterrorist teams worldwide. MP5 refers purely to the model number." With an open palm he slapped the black polycarbonate butt. "A2 is the fixed stock model. The A3 version, which Level One carry, has a retractable stock which makes vehicle work concealment much easier; in fact it cuts down length from twenty-seven inches to nineteen."

I raised my hand. "Excuse me, Staff, but why don't Level Two carry those?"

"F*** knows, Sarge. Probably because the stocks cost about a hundred and fifty quid each," he squeaked. "These weapons are nine millimeter, taking the same bog-standard round as the Glock. To the media and many other people, these are often referred to as sub-machine-guns; we, however, have replaced the safety lever and adapted them to fire single shot only." He paused to draw breath. "However, other rapid-fire and silenced versions are available to us. With its unique design this weapon unloaded weighs only 5.59 pounds [2.5kg]; with a thirty-round magazine capacity, it is accurate to well over fifty metres but, make no bones about it fellas, the nine millimeter round we use in this and the Glock is more than capable of ripping through skin, tissue and bone at that distance. And with its jacketed soft point, hopefully it will dump its energy and not over-penetrate. Don't ever underestimate your weapon or ammunition." (Collins 1997: 33–34)

Initially, the Metropolitan Police D11 acquired select-fire MP5 SMGs in late 1977 but they were used only in situations against heavily armed criminals or when escorting convoys carrying valuable loads or dangerous criminals to court (Smith 2013: 47–48). At the time Collins was describing, Level One referred primarily to the instructors who, in effect, acted as a SWAT team and would be deployed to siege or hostage incidents. Level Two referred to trained firearms officers who handled other assignments requiring armed police. In 1991, Level One and Level Two officers were merged to form Specialist Firearms Officers (SFOs). A police officer had to pass an intensive course to be rated an SFO. A lot of the training was in tactical operations in buildings and through realistic live-fire exercises. There are also Authorized Firearms Officers (AFOs), who are the crews of the ARVs. In a barricade or hostage situation, the ARV crews, who would normally be first on the scene, would set up a perimeter to contain the situation. Once trained, SFO officers were on standby in case of callouts and could call on a van carrying equipment that might needed in a barricade or hostage situation.

Collins relates various incidents in which the MP5s were used to good effect by the SFOs. In one incident two armed criminals, one disguised as a police officer, had taken a hostage during a botched robbery:

With a sneer on his face and still holding his captive Charalambous raised the self-loader, pointing it squarely at my chest. People that have been in similar traumatic circumstances will often tell you that time appears to slow down – and this was certainly my

An armed Metropolitan Police officer on duty on Westminster Bridge, London. His weapon is an MP5-SFA2. (© Mark Richardson / Alamy)

experience. In the split second that followed, I took in not only his expression, but thought how ridiculous he looked in fancy dress. As I waited for the impact, unable to fire for fear of hitting the guard, I wondered whether he would hit the grenade, causing me to explode in the middle of Crouch Hill in a spectacular display of green smoke. I also thought of Joe, high above in his lair behind me, poised, finger on trigger and cross-hairs on my back.

That was enough. In one movement I sprang backward behind cover, accompanied by the sharp crack of gunfire. No more than a fraction of a second later, there were screams all around me as more shots followed. I was back on the pavement in an instant, witnessing the tumbling form of the "joke" cop as he spiralled towards the floor, and away from the guard. Nigel, to my left, had gasped the opportunity. Bringing to bear the MP5 he had instinctively fired a pair. His sense of direction – the ability to hit a target without aiming, taught extensively by SO19 for close-range work – causing the rounds to hit Charalambous in the chest and spinning him. With the weapon in his hand he was still a threat, so Nigel had fired two more rounds at the falling man. (Collins 1997: 180–81)

This incident is a good example of SFO training, which inculcated the use of "double taps" to make sure that a suspect was stopped. Within the last few years, AFOs (Armed Firearms Officers) including those assigned to ARVs (Armed Response Vehicles) have received a week of training on the Glock 17 pistol and MP5 carbine along with six weeks of high-speed driving and other vehicle operations. They periodically receive additional training. AFOs who become Specialist Firearms Officers undergo another eight weeks of training, which in addition to weapons use focuses on tactics for hostage rescue and armed search.

A major change in policy occurred in 1986 when D11 officers were deployed to Heathrow Airport carrying their MP5 SMGs openly (Smith 2013: 78). Once specialized airport officers were trained they were armed with the MP5 semi-automatic carbine. MP5K SMGs were available to armed officers including those assigned to diplomatic or royal protection. Although armed Metropolitan Police officers normally used the MP5K primarily on dignitary protection assignments, in October 1991, six officers armed with MP5Ks were deployed to the Turks and Caicos islands to help guard Pablo Escobar's brother-in-law until he could be extradited to the USA. It was feared that there would an attempt either to rescue him or to assassinate him to keep him from revealing information (Smith 2013: 109).

The Kennedy ERT

The Kennedy Space Center's Emergency Response Team (ERT) has been a noteworthy user of the MP5 for a couple of reasons. Currently the ERT uses HK 416 assault rifles, though the unit retains the MP5 for some specialized duties. Initially, members of the unit were charged with protecting the Space Shuttle (when it was still operational), as well as the personnel and facilities of the Space Center, a mission they still have. A friend of the author's was in charge of security at Kennedy Space Center at one point and once explained one use of the MP5 during a launch. Members of the ERT armed with MP5s were deployed to various points around the Center from which a threat analysis had determined a sniper with a .50-caliber rifle might be able to hit the shuttle during a launch. By interdicting those locations, the ERT denied them to terrorists. As a sidenote, a friend of the author's once told him that the swampy areas within the Space Center perimeter were hard for the ERT to secure, but that the large number of alligators living there offered pretty good interdiction!

The second reason the Kennedy ERT's MP5s are noteworthy is that they proved the weapon's durability. In his book, *Heckler & Koch's MP5 Submachine Gun*, Frank James points out that one Kennedy Space Center MP5 – among the first MP5s obtained by the Center – fired 571,600 rounds between 1984 and 1990. During that time some small parts needed to be replaced, but this was done in the armory during normal servicing. Since during that period, each member of the ERT fired 15,000–18,000 rounds through the MP5 every year in training, the number of rounds fired added up quickly. Additionally, other members of the Kennedy Space Center Security Force shoot a substantial number of rounds through the MP5 every year. At the Center's range, records were kept on each MP5, detailing rounds fired and maintenance performed. According to James, the records he examined were for one of three MP5s used for training. The 571,600 rounds figure is based on the point at which the barrel had worn out. James states that with installation of a new barrel, the weapon could have probably remained in service, but the cost of having HK install a new barrel and refurbish it was close to the cost of a new weapon, so it was removed from service (James 2000: 163–67).

August 2006: Massachusetts State Troopers assigned to security at Logan Airport, Boston, patrol with MP5 SMGs. Since two of the hijacked airliners on September 11 came from Logan, the Massachusetts State Police take security there especially seriously. (© JESSICA RINALDI/ Reuters/Corbis)

Other law-enforcement users

The MP5 has seen wide use among an array of special police units, including: Belarus's ALMAZ counterterrorist unit, Canada's Royal Canadian Mounted Police, Costa Rica's UEI (Unidad Especial de Intervencion, or "Special Intervention Unit"), Greece's EKAM (Eidiki Katastaltiki Antitromokratiki Monada, or "Special Counter-Terrorist Unit"), Kenya's police, Liechtenstein's police, Luxembourg's Unité Spéciale de la Police (Special Unit of the Police), the New Zealand Police Special Tactics Group, the Philippines' National Police Special Action Force, the Singapore Police STAR unit, the South African Police Special Task Force, Spain's Grupo Especial de Operaciones (Special Group of Operations; GEO), and the Police Service of Northern Ireland.

The MP5 and patrol duties

The MP5 has also achieved a measure of popularity with police units that carry out normal patrol duties. For example, many German police agencies have MP5s in patrol vehicles to supplement the handguns carried by officers. Although the standard patrol-car long gun for most US law-enforcement agencies is either the 5.56×45mm carbine or the shotgun, at least some have used the MP5 as a patrol-car weapon. The author remembers one municipal department, which was virtually surrounded by the city of Detroit. Patrol cars were equipped with MP5s, due to the likelihood of officers having to deal with violent crime spilling into their jurisdiction. In many cases, when the MP5 is used by US police agencies in patrol vehicles, the full-auto feature is locked out or the weapons are semi-auto only, and they function only as semi-auto carbines. In many cases, supervisor's cars or SWAT team members will have select-fire MP5s.

As great as the MP5's popularity has been among law-enforcement agencies, that popularity has been eroded somewhat over the last decade as more agencies have started using rifle-caliber carbines for the same missions. The carbine offers greater range, striking power, and penetration, yet when loaded with proper ammunition does not overpenetrate. Nevertheless, the MP5 remains one of the most widely used law-enforcement weapons in the world.

A very compact, blowback-operated SMG beloved by filmmakers for its aggressive appearance, the MAC-10 was developed in 1964 by Gordon Ingram. The use of a telescoping bolt allowed the MAC-10 to be kept to a very short overall length and balanced the weapon over the pistol grip. MAC-10s were chambered in 9×19mm or .45 ACP caliber. The MAC-10 with Sionics suppressor, designed so it could also function as a foregrip, was widely used by US intelligence and special-operations personnel during the 1970s. Ingram added a strap beneath the muzzle to aid in controlling the unsuppressed MAC-10; since the MAC-10 had a cyclic rate of 1,090rds/min in 9×19mm and 1,145rds/min in .45 ACP, this strap offered some counter to muzzle rise. The law-enforcement or military units of more than a dozen countries in addition to the United States have used the MAC-10. (Author)

THE MP5 IN MILITARY SERVICE

The SAS

Though GSG 9's rescue in Mogadishu was a great success, it was Operation *Nimrod*, the rescue of hostages at the Iranian Embassy in London on May 5, 1980, that made the MP5 the most recognized counterterrorist weapon in the world. However, the MP5 was not the original choice of the SAS Special Projects (SP) Team. Initially, the Ingram MAC-10 was used, but after the SAS had shot the MP5 while doing cross-training with GSG 9, the HK gun was chosen. The author can attest from using the MAC-10 and the MP5 that there is no comparison when surgical precision is needed. The MP5 was definitely the correct choice for hostage-rescue operations.

Before the MP5 had its moment in the world spotlight at Princes Gate, SAS troops had spent many long hours honing their skills with the weapon. Michael Paul Kennedy, one of the members of the assault team at the embassy, describes some of the training:

> As I pulled on my assault kit, a pain in my temple throbbed continuously ... I drew on my skin-tight aviators' leather gloves, cocked the action of my Heckler Koch MP5, introducing a live round into the chamber, applied the safety catch, carried out the same operation on my Browning pistol and realized I had begun to sweat. It was going to be a long, tedious day.
>
> "... The game plan is the same. Head shots – double taps or single only. Limits of exploitation are your allocated rooms." He [the instructor] pointed to the blackboard, circling every individual's responsibility with the barrel of his 9-milly. "Be on your doors in five minutes. I will initiate with a burst of fire into the long gallery. Any questions?"
>
> ... The combination of the twenty-round burst from the MP5 and the deafening explosion of the thunderflash on the ISFE [instantaneous safety-fuse, electric] rocked the killing house. My number three on the Remington blasted the lock of the small combat room with a blank cartridge and then kicked the door in ... as the door flew open. In I went and headed straight for the cluster of figure-eleven targets propped up in their rickety stands in the far corner. Usual thing, I thought quickly, my eyes doing a radar scan of the room. Four terrorists and three hostages.
>
> Ba ... Bang, Ba ... Bang, Ba ... Bang. Three double taps in less than three seconds, six neat holes in three terrorist heads.
>
> Ba ... Bang, My number two neutralized a kneeling target behind the chair in a corner. (Kennedy 1989: 175–76)

As good as the MP5 is, it took endless hours of practice on the range and in the killing house – a building designed to allow live-fire training in hostage rescue and building clearing – for members of the SAS to perfect the teamwork it took to clear a room of terrorists safely, quickly and surely and without killing hostages. They had to learn the precision weapon handling to wield the MP5 to maximum effect. And the members of the

One of the light mounts used by the SAS during the 1980 Iranian Embassy siege at Princes Gate, London. (Author)

SAS would need all their skills, for during the training exercise described above, their beepers went off to alert them to the mission at the Iranian Embassy in London. "Blue Team" as used by the authors refers to the fact that the SP Team was divided into a Red Team and a Blue Team during its time as the Regiment's counterterrorist element. One team would be training and on standby while the other team would be the alert team for immediate deployment if an incident arose. Both Red and Blue Teams were deployed to Princes Gate, with one ready for an immediate assault if hostages were killed and the other team resting. In the event, both teams took part in the actual assault. In *Go! Go! Go!* the preparations of the SP Team for the Embassy takedown, including their MP5s, are described:

> The SP Team's seven white-painted Range Rovers and its motley collection of Ford Transit vans were parked in a neat row along the far side of the two hangers. A pallet loaded with equipment for immediate use sat directly behind each Range Rover. It included boxes of operational ammunition; operational weapons such as Remington 870 pump shotguns, MP5 machine guns, Polecat gas-canister launchers and British Army-issue hand grenades; food supplies; water; tool-rolls; radios and spare batteries; model S6 gas respirators; night-vision goggles; boxes of CS and stun grenades; medical equipment; method-of-entry kit; and – although there weren't enough of them to go round each member of the team – Maglite MP5 gun-torches on permanent charge ready to be picked up prior to departure.
>
> All team members had a green army-issue holdall bag that travelled with them in the operational vehicles. It held their gloves, NBC hood, balaclava, S6 respirator, coveralls, boots, belt kit, ops waistcoat, weapon-cleaning kit, 4 by 2 body armour and ceramic plates for body armour, and abseiling essentials. The bag also held personal weapons like the MP5 and 9mm Browning semi-automatic pistol and a couple of shell dressings; not to mention four MP5 thirty-round magazines and one twenty-round magazine, two twelve-round mags for the Browning, and individual operational ammunition. That meant as soon as they got to an incident they could be operational in a matter of minutes. (Firmin & Pearson 2011: 21)

When the authors state that the each SAS operator carried one 20-round magazine in his holdall, they are probably referring to the 15-round magazine, as 20-round magazines were not available for the MP5. It is possible that they are referring to a 20-round extension magazine for the Browning pistol, which was sometimes used by the SAS. Also, when they state that the Browning magazines held 12 rounds, this is incorrect. The magazine held 13 rounds, but SAS troops were trained to load only 12 rounds. In the book, it is noted, too, that the SAS found the lack of weapons lights for all of the MP5s a disadvantage in the smoke, dust, and gas-filled darkened rooms, though there had been repeated appeals to the Ministry of Defence (MOD) for more.

The SAS team was deployed to a position near the Iranian Embassy to be ready to assault in case the terrorists began killing hostages. On May

OPPOSITE
A member of the SAS SP Team around the time of the Princes Gate assault armed with his HK MP5. He wears his Browning Hi-Power semi-automatic pistol on his right thigh and spare MP5 magazines on his left thigh. Note that he carries a spare Browning magazine on his left wrist. He also wears the anti-flash hood and respirator. (Author's collection)

Members of the SAS carry out an entry at Princes Gate armed with HK MP5s; note that the man in the left foreground has a light mounted above the SMG, rather than below in standard HK fashion. (Author's collection)

5, the sixth day of the siege, a hostage was killed and dumped in front of the embassy. At that point the SAS assault team made sure their MP5s were cleaned and oiled, then loaded and ready for action. As Michael Paul Kennedy notes, the SAS operators knew they would need speed, surprise, and aggression to clear the 50 rooms of the embassy. He considered the advice of Paddy Mayne, one of the founders of the SAS: "When you enter a room full of armed men, shoot the first person who makes a move, hostile or otherwise. He has started to think and is therefore dangerous …" (Kennedy 1989: 192).

Although in the hurry to achieve the mission Kennedy initially fired a burst of 20 rounds into a dustbin – apparently, his adrenalin was flowing and he was expecting to encounter terrorists as he moved – the assault team quickly cleared the embassy, firing their HKs with deadly effect. In one case, Kennedy could not fire at a terrorist clutching a grenade for fear of hitting other members of the SAS, so he used the butt of the MP5 on the terrorist's neck, letting other operators shoot him with their MP5s as he fell clear (Kennedy 1989: 196). Other members of the assault group used their MP5s in the way intended as they terminally double-tapped four terrorists. A fifth terrorist was killed by a sniper in Hyde Park (Scholey 1999: 215). All the terrorists but one were killed. The MP5 proved very effective in assaulting the Iranian Embassy, but since both the Red and Blue SP Teams had to be ready to carry out an immediate assault, the supply of MP5s was stretched. In *Go! Go! Go!*, it is noted that:

The Regiment [the SAS] had adopted the MP5 about three years before. This had changed the whole game in favor of the good guys. For Special Forces everywhere, the MP5 was a Rolls-Royce weapon.

Most men had the basic model. A few had the MP5-K, Kurz ("short" in German); two of the Blue reserve team had the MP5-SD, or silenced version: but only because there weren't enough of the basic model to go round.

Far more accurate out to 300 metres than the Sterling SMG it replaced, the MP5 had a rolling-locked bolt system [*sic*], making it quicker, easier, and safer to fire. Its magazine, which came in fifteen or thirty-round variants projected downwards, not sideways, which helped to prevent misfires, and the spent shells ejected sideways and not down.

The sighting system on the MP5 was also a huge improvement on the Sterling's. Based on the principle of concentric rings, which channel human eyesight naturally, the MP5 had a rotary drum rear sight and a hooded post fore sight. Along with its many other merits, the weapon was superbly engineered; it tolerated not being cleaned as much as it should be, and it was very reliable.

When it came to ammo, the SP team – like the rest of the Regiment – chambered full metal jacketed Mk.2Z 9×19mm NATO standard Parabellum rounds in both the MP5 and Browning High-Power semi-automatic pistol standard close assault weapons. (Firmin & Pearson 2011: 23–24)

When comparing the Sterling to the MP5, the authors make an important point about the Sterling's magazines, which projected sideways. The Sterling magazines would have been far more likely to catch on doorways or other projections when the gun was in confined spaces, unlike the MP5's downward-projecting magazine.

Rusty Firmin, one of the authors of *Go! Go! Go!*, was actually a member of the SAS assault team at the Iranian Embassy. It is interesting to note the description of the MP5's advantages, since this information most likely came from him. Firman and Pearson also discuss how the MP5 was used as a "master key" during the Embassy assault:

Pete S. turned the doorknob and yanked it back. The door was locked. He lifted the nose of the MP5, pointed it at the lock and opened fire. The lock disintegrated. Booting the door open, he looked inside ...

Room 9's left-hand door led out onto the landing and stairwell. Palmer and Red Team leader were already trying to get through it. But anticipating just such an attack route, the gunmen had locked that door as well. Raising his MP5, Palmer put a burst into the lock. It shattered, taking a large section of the solid oak panelling with it ... (Firmin & Pearson 2011: 173)

A point to note is that it is specified in the account that the door was left-hand opening. During the preparation for a building assault, knowing which way doors open – in/out, right/left – is critical, as this knowledge can shave off vital seconds as operators move through a building.

A close-up of the trigger group for an MP5K showing four positions – safe (single white bullet), semi-auto (single red bullet), three-round-burst (three red bullets), and full-auto (seven red bullets with open-ended box). (C&S)

Reportedly, at Princes Gate SAS operator Tommy Palmer had an MP5 malfunction when the gun fed a faulty cartridge, resulting in a "dead man's click." A terrorist fired two shots at him, which missed. Palmer allowed his MP5 to drop onto its sling and transitioned to his Browning, but the terrorist had fled into the telex room where there were hostages. As Palmer burst into the room he saw the terrorist with a grenade in his hand and killed him with a single headshot from his Browning (Firmin & Pearson 2011: 194–95).

14th Intelligence Company

The MP5 was used to good effect in other British military units, including 14th Intelligence Company, which carried out surveillance and gathered intelligence in Northern Ireland. Unlike most special-forces units, 14th Intelligence Company had female operators who received intensive weapons training. One of the female members, writing under the pseudonym "Jackie George," describes the value of the MP5K in *She Who Dares*:

> For the next two weeks we continued with our weapons training. We learned about the MP5K, a short, stocky machine pistol favoured by the SAS and used to great effect during the Iranian Embassy siege. It was a strange-looking weapon that could fire single or multiple bursts.
>
> On the first day Brian and Bruce showed us how to strip the weapon, how it worked and all the important safety drills. We were told that over the water [in Northern Ireland] we would be carrying an MP5K along with another rifle in our vehicles and that we would have a pistol in our belts. We practised double tapping with the MP5K on the ranges. It was deadly accurate and we were surprised by the lack of recoil.
>
> The most important thing now was to practise car drills. At first we were in pairs, the passenger using the MP5K to lay down initial fire, with the driver relying on his pistol. In a real contact situation the driver would not have time to reach behind him for his other weapon. Then the fun began when we practised in fours, with three of us using MP5Ks. In the heat of the moment it was easy to slip the catch from single to multiple shot and empty a thirty-round magazine within two

seconds. Care also had to be taken as we ran back towards our cars, crossing each other's line of fire. (George 1999: 89)

It is likely that "Ms George" is confusing the MP5K with the MP5A2 used at Princes Gate. However, in *Go! Go! Go!* Firmin and Pearson do note that a few operators at Princes Gate did have MP5Ks (Firmin & Pearson 2011: 22). In fact, one of the two injuries to members of the SAS was sustained by an operator who was using an early MP5K that lacked the protrusion on the handguard to keep the hand from sliding forward in front of the barrel. As a result, the soldier put a crease in one of his fingers while firing (Firmin & Pearson 2011: 211).

The MP5K was especially well suited to the clandestine surveillance mission of 14th Intelligence Company, as it could easily be concealed beneath a coat and could be handled well within the confines of a vehicle, while still giving the operators a substantial amount of firepower. Later in the book, "George" illustrates the concealability of the compact MP5K on operations. On an operation in Northern Ireland in which "George" and another female operator were tasked with shadowing an off-duty soldier targeted for assassination, she states:

> Tony and I ran a circuit around the fish and chip shop checking the hedgerows for any sign of an IRA ambush. I was dressed in a tracksuit with my pistol strapped tightly to my waist and a radio rubbing against my bare skin. I was also carrying a small haversack on my back that contained an MP5K. Becky and her partner were on standby to take over from us after a couple of hours. (George 1999: 161)

On another occasion, during a previous tour in Northern Ireland, "George" relates that she and her partner were on an operation when they saw armed men on the moor and a suspicious car approaching. When the car stopped and men with rifles got out, George grabbed her MP5K and her partner seized his HK53. They leapt from the car pointing their weapons ready to engage – she had already released the safety – when it turned out to be

Instead of the MP5 some 14th Intelligence Company operators used the HK53, the compact version of the HK33 5.56×45mm NATO assault rifle, which offered greater stopping power yet was still relatively concealable. (HK USA)

other members of their unit along with some SAS operators (George 1999:113–14). It was a good illustration that sometimes good training not only teaches an operator when to shoot but also when to hold fire until a situation is clear! Although "George" never had to fire her MP5K or HK53 at terrorists in Northern Ireland, it was a constant companion that would have evened the odds had she and her partner been spotted.

A member of Poland's Jednostka Wojskowa Formoza (Military Unit Formoza) combat-swimmer unit comes ashore with his HK MP5A3 SMG, which has a SureFire forearm with integral light and an EOTech holographic sight. (Author's collection)

The SBS

The MP5 also proved a weapon very well suited to some of the missions of the SBS. For oilrig or ship assaults, the MP5 was sufficiently compact that it could be used in confined spaces or during boarding missions. On some oilrig assaults, the SBS troopers were inserted from a submarine, in which a long rifle would have been much more likely to impede exiting. The 9×19mm round was not as likely to overpenetrate as a rifle round, either. Overpenetration could cause explosions or fire from hitting machinery and could also penetrate a compartment containing hostages of crew members. The MP5SD was especially useful for oilrig or ship actions. The suppressor lowered the noise level of firing, meaning that that terrorists would be less likely to know what was happening elsewhere on the vessel or rig, and making SBS communications easier in steel-walled environments that would greatly magnify the sound of unmuted gunshots. Additionally, the suppressed SMG would lower the amount of muzzle flash, so there would be less chance of igniting flammable materials likely to be encountered on these missions. Members of the SBS also took MP5SDs to the Falklands for use to eliminate Argentine sentries during raids (Camsell 2000: 170).

In *Black Water*, Don Camsell discusses the preparation for a practice assault on a North Sea oil rig, including preparing his MP5 for action:

To survive in the North Sea we wore "woolly bears," thick thermal suits that would keep us just the right side of frozen while we sat on top of a submarine doing 15 knots under water. On top of this came a waterproof lightweight dry bag; this enabled us to swim and climb with relative ease and comfort. Lightweight boots were next, followed by the weapons holster which carried the 9mm Sig-Sauer pistol and four magazines with four more for the HK. The holster could also fit a diving knife, or you could secure it on your arm or leg. This equipment fitted so tightly to the body that you can't bend freely until you are in the water – then it stretches. Over this comes the "waistcoat" which carries the day and night flare, another four HK magazines (we were ready to start a small war here), a strobe light, plasticuffs (we do take prisoners), a waterproof VHF multi-channel radio, a SARBE (search and rescue beacon emergency), and individual aide-memoire.

We carried an HKMP5A3 9mm sub-machine gun on top of the waistcoat, attached by a weapon slung on the right or left side of the body depending on whether you were right- or left-handed. It was secured to the body through the trigger guard by a karabiner. It was fitted with a loaded magazine and a round up the spout, safety catch applied. The last items to load on were the LAR 5 [attack oxygen-breathing apparatus] and a life jacket. Now we really looked the part: the Men in Black, ready to protect the country from the scum of wherever. (Camsell 2000: 17)

There are some noteworthy points here. First, the SBS operators carry a great deal of ammunition – five full magazines (one in the pistol) for the SIG and nine full magazines (one in the SMG) for the MP5. Strictly speaking, the MP5 magazines would not be loaded with the full 30 rounds, as experienced operators learn to load 28 or 29 rounds so that the magazine could be inserted into the magazine well with the bolt closed. The SBS might also load one less round in the 15-round SIG P-226 magazine. Because compact weapons are better for the SBS's missions, the MP5A3 with folding stock was chosen. Carrying the MP5A3 with both the sling and the additional karabiner also suited the SBS mission, to reduce the chances of losing the weapon when swimming, canoeing, or climbing.

The MP5 is known for its reliability, but all operators must practice for weapon failures, requiring them to take immediate action. They need to adopt well-rehearsed malfunction drills to clear jams or quickly transition to their pistol. Camsell describes going through his mental checklist before an operation:

> Above all: do I know my drills? If my Heckler and Koch gets a stoppage, will I deal with it quickly enough not to endanger myself or my team. (The trick is to work out within a second whether you can clear it or whether you should drop it and draw your Sig-Sauer pistol – take any longer to make up your mind up and you might be dead.) And it does come to shooting, will the ammunition work? (Camsell 2000: 12)

Ammunition choice is always important for members of combat-swimmer units, who will spend a substantial amount of time with their weapons and magazines submerged. Camsell reflects on the decisions behind transitioning to his pistol. It should be pointed out that under the stress of combat, operators may lose track of how many rounds have been fired; hence, first it is important to check that the "malfunction" is not just an empty magazine. The MP5's lack of a bolt hold-open device when a magazine is empty makes it necessary to pull the bolt rearward manually to check for an empty magazine, or to detach the magazine and check it. One failure procedure, in the case of a stoppage not apparently caused by a failure to feed or extract, is to lock the bolt back, drop the magazine, and immediately insert a new magazine and slap the bolt to let it go forward.

The US Navy SEALs

As with the SBS, the US Navy SEALs found the MP5 especially well suited to Maritime Anti-Terrorism (MAT) operations. However, it was not easy convincing the naval hierarchy to purchase the German-made SMG. In his book *Rogue Warrior*, Richard Marcinko, the first commander of SEAL Team Six, describes his difficulties in obtaining the MP5. He reports a

conversation he had with the US Navy commodore in charge of approving SEAL Team Six purchases:

> Next I bought German Heckler & Koch MP5, 9mm submachine guns. He complained again. "Why foreign guns? We can get MAC10s for a third of the price."
>
> "Because the HKs are better, Ted. They're more accurate. They're more consistent. They adapt well to our mission."
>
> "I'm dead set against it."
>
> He called his rabbis, and I called mine. SEAL Team Six got HKs. (Marcinko 1992: 268–69)

The conversation Marcinko reports took place a few months after the SAS had famously used the MP5 against the terrorists who had seized the Iranian Embassy. However, since the commodore with whom Marcinko was dealing was outside the special-operations community, he had no idea of the capabilities of the MP5. A decade later, when the present author was training US military personnel in general-officer protection and hostage-rescue tactics, he found it quite useful when higher-ranking officers stopped by to observe the training to give them a chance to shoot the MP5. At that time it was still issued only to special-operations units, but it had developed a cachet. After firing the MP5, the officers usually left feeling a little more "martial" and more satisfied with the training their troops were getting.

SEALs versus Somali pirates (previous pages)

Since 2009 at least, but possibly earlier, a number of elite US naval units have been detached to naval task forces operating as part of NATO forces in the Gulf of Aden off the coast of Somalia. Members of the US Navy SEALs and US Marine Corps special-warfare units have the mission of carrying out boarding operations of suspected pirate vessels and of rescuing hostages. The best-known operation by the US Navy SEALs was carried out on April 12, 2009, when three Somali pirates holding the caption of the *Maersk Alabama* were killed by snipers from SEAL Team Six, allowing the captain to be rescued. The SEALs are also trained to carry out combat boarding operations from helicopters, fast rubber boats, or by swimming to the target vessel underwater.

The SEALs shown here have boarded a vessel after swimming to it, as indicated by their wetsuits. Before climbing the scaling ladder they have taken off their swimming fins and attached them to their gear for more freedom of movement. They have also removed the mouthpiece of their breathing apparatus, but have retained their goggles to offer eye protection. Normally, the first man over a rail will be armed with a pistol, as with the figure at the right, to allow him to keep one hand free for grasping the rail. The pistol is the SIG P-226 Navy model used by the SEALs.

Presumably, the other SEAL had already cleared the rail and transitioned to his HK MP5N and has engaged the pirate who was raising his AK-47. Note that the SEAL has two MP5 magazines linked to allow a more rapid combat magazine change. From the number of empty cases visible, he has his MP5N set on full-auto rather than burst mode, which is an option on the SEALs' version of the MP5.

Once adopted, the MP5 soon proved itself with the SEALs. In his book *Seal Team Six*, Howard E. Wisdin describes the preparations he and other SEALs from SEAL Team Two made aboard the carrier USS *John F. Kennedy* prior to an assault on a ship laying mines during Operation *Desert Storm*:

US Navy SEALs training to take down a ship; the SEAL kneeling in the foreground is armed with an HK MP5-N. Because of the ambidextrous safety on the MP5-N, left-handed firing is easier, because the safety may be accessed with the thumb of the left hand rather than having to operate a safety designed for a right-handed shooter by shifting the trigger finger. Note that the SEAL has two magazines linked. (US Navy)

We geared up, wearing black BDUs. On our feet we wore Adidas GSG9 assault boots. They're soft on the bottom and grip well, like wearing a tennis shoe with ankle support. You can get them wet and fins slip on easily over the tops. To this day, that's my favorite boot. Black balaclavas covered our heads, and paint covered our exposed skins. For our hands, we customized our green aviator gloves by dying them black, then cutting off two of the fingers on the right-hand glove: the trigger finger down to the second knuckle and the thumb down to the first knuckle. With the fingers cut out, it became easier to squeeze the trigger, change magazines, pull the pin on flashbangs, etc. Casio watches on our wrists kept time. On my belt, in the small of my back, sat a gas mask. During Desert Storm, everyone prepared for gas or biological weapons; Hussein was reported to still have chemical weapons that he wouldn't hesitate to use.

I carried the Heckler & Koch MP-5 submachine gun with a SIG Sauer 9mm on my right hip. I kept a thirty-round magazine in the MP-5. Some guys like to carry two magazines in the weapon, but our experience was that the double magazine limited our maneuverability, and it's hard to do a magazine change. I carried three magazines on my left thigh and an extra three in my backpack. We test-fired our weapons off the fantail, on the back of the ship. (Wisdin & Templin 2011: 124–25)

The SEALs successfully boarded the ship and secured it. Although there were a couple of times it appeared they might have to fire their MP5s, it did not prove necessary; once the ship was secured it was turned over the US Coast Guard personnel to be taken to a friendly port in the Red Sea. As with all of their weapons, the SEALs train intensively to master the MP5:

That evening, Petty Officer Will Gautier is in front of Class 2-02. "Gentlemen, tonight we're going to introduce you to the H&K MP5A. Guys, you're gonna love this submachine gun. It can do a lot of things. In the teams we use it primarily for ship boarding and close-quarters battle."

... The next day, the members of Class 2-02 are back on the range. They have their SIG Sauer pistols strapped to one thigh and magazine pouches strapped to the other; fifteen-round magazines for the SIG and thirty-round magazines for the MP5. After a round of familiarization fire with the MP5, they begin combat shooting drills. They are taught to use the ring-and-hooded sights on the MP5. If the sight picture is

US Navy SEALs firing their MP5s from behind barricades during tactical training. Note that the SEAL at left is firing from his right shoulder, which requires him to expose much more of his body. This is why firing from the left shoulder when firing from the left side of a barricade is desirable. (US Navy)

there the rounds go through the target. As with the pistols, they begin with a single target, then begin double-tapping individual targets – two rounds on the same target. Compared to the SIG, the MP5 is easy to use and accurate. The men practice changing magazines on the MP5, then they transition from the submachine gun to the SIG. In the afternoon, they continue on the stress courses – competitive shooting drills where accuracy and speed both count. The MP5 stress course is run two by two, so the other students must be aware of the targets and their shooting partners. (Couch 2004: 71–72)

The SEALs use competition between the two shooters to add stress to the exercise, with the loser often having to perform runs or other physical training. The author once witnessed SEALs training with their weapons at the Blackwater training facility in North Carolina. Operators were shooting at steel plates representing hostages and hostage-takers. As part of the exercise, any SEAL who hit a hostage target or missed a terrorist target had to run carrying one of the heavy steel targets. Not only did this add an incentive to shoot straight, but it helped build the upper-body strength so important in many SEAL missions.

Note also that the SEAL instructor delineates the special missions for which the SEALs normally use the MP5 – combat boarding and CQB. Although most special-operations units and counterterrorist units retain the MP5 in the armory, many now use short-barreled carbines such as the US M4 or the HK G36K. These carbines are still very compact but fire the rifle-caliber 5.56×45mm NATO round, which gives the operator the option of engaging more effectively at longer distance and of penetrating body armor that the 9×19mm round would not punch through. The usual criticism of the carbine for hostage rescue is that the round may overpenetrate, but specialized frangible rounds are now available. Units that now use the M4 or G36K as their primary weapon are generally units in which operators are trained to use a variety of weapons to suit the missions, and, thus the MP5 remains one tool in their toolbox.

A GIGN counterterrorist operator firing an MP5K, without a stock. GIGN liked the MP5K without stock as it could be readily concealed and handled in tight spaces, such as an aircraft cabin. The MP5K, especially as used by GIGN without a stock, requires substantial skill to use it effectively. GIGN operators practiced with it enough that they could handle it well. (Author's collection)

JTF2

Another unit that adopted the MP5 was Canada's Joint Task Force Two (JTF2), which was formed in 1993 and given the counterterrorist mission. According to David Pugliese, the MP5, favored by counterterrorism units worldwide, was selected as the unit's main firearm (Pugliese 2002: 30). Pugliese goes into more detail about the use of the MP5 by JTF2:

These members of the Royal Canadian Mounted Police's ERT are armed with the MP5A3. Their SMGs mount weapon lights and EOTech Holographic sights. (Author's collection)

> Like many special-operations units, JTF2 relies heavily on the Heckler and Koch family of MP-5 sub-machine guns. The German-made 9mm weapons have a well-deserved reputation for reliability. Designed in

These members of DYK, the Greek Navy's special-warfare unit, are armed with MP5SDs, presumably made by Ellinika Amyntika Systimata (Hellenic Defense Systems; EAS). (US Navy)

the 1960s, the MP-5 allows the operator to fire semi-automatically or full-auto simply by flipping the selector switch on the receiver. The 9mm bullet is considered easier to handle than the 5.56mm or .45 ACP calibres as the recoil is very moderate. As an added feature, Heckler and Koch has a twin magazine clamp that allows the shooter to carry two magazines on the gun to enable quick magazine changes in a combat situation. MP-5s have either a 15 or 30-round magazine and can be field-striped [*sic*] in [a] matter of seconds without tools. Unlike most sub-machineguns, the MP-5 fires from a closed bolt. This helps increase accuracy as there is no forward movement of the bolt when the trigger is pulled (which in other sub-machineguns can put the weapon slightly off target).

JTF2 uses the MP-5A2 (fixed stock), MP-5A3 (collapsing stock), and the MP-5SD (suppressed, either fixed or folding stock). The standard weight of the MP-5 is three kilograms and it has a cyclic rate of fire of 800 rounds per minute. The SD version uses a built-in suppressor or "silencer" to muffle the sound of the gun's report. In that system, the barrel is encased in a suppressor tube; escaping gases are diverted through the aluminum ports inside the suppressor, causing a drop in the bullet's normal velocity. As a result, when the bullet leaves the muzzle it is traveling at a subsonic speed and the sound being emitted is similar to a loud hiss of air. Maintenance for the silencer is simple and involves using a cleansing agent to rinse out gunpowder residue that has built up in the device over time. The other MP-5 variant commonly used by counter-terrorist teams is the MP-5K, a shortened, easily concealed machinegun. It is not known if that weapon is in JTF2's arsenal. (Pugliese 2002: 126)

As practiced by many other counterterrorist units, JTF2 uses Simunition to do live-fire training with their MP5s. An incident related by Pugliese illustrates why even highly trained units must take great care not to mix training ammunition with live ammunition:

In November, 1999, a JTF2 soldier put two live rounds into an MP-5 sub-machinegun during exercises that required simulation ammunition. The MP-5 had been outfitted with a simulation barrel device, an insert that fits into the machinegun. When the real bullet was fired it blew the simulation insert from the barrel and across the room. There were no injuries. A military police investigation determined that the incident was an accident and no range procedures had been broken. The JTF2 soldier involved was not punished. (Pugliese 2002: 148)

Presumably the author means "Simunition" rather than "Simulation." Also, although it is claimed that "no range procedures had been broken," they should have been. Prior to carrying out Simunition exercises, all personnel should be inspected to make sure that live ammunition has not been brought into the training area.

Other military users

Examples of MP5 users are myriad, as somewhere around 100 countries use it for their military or police. Even countries that traditionally use domestically produced weapons, such as France and Russia, have adopted the MP5. The French have proved to be especially fond of the MP5K, as this model has been used by Groupe d'intervention de la Gendarmerie Nationale (National Gendarmerie Intervention Group; GIGN, formed in 1973) and – carried in briefcases – Groupe de Sécurité de la Présidence de la République (Security Group of the President of the Republic; GSPR, formed in 1983), the French presidential protection unit.

Many military units have found, as have the SBS and the SEALs, that the MP5 lends itself especially well to some NSW missions. Among such units are: Australia's Tactical Assault Groups; the Bangladesh Navy's Special Warfare Diving and Salvage (SWADS) unit; Canadian Forces Naval Boarding Parties; Denmark's Frømandskorpset (Frogman Corps); the *Kampfschwimmer* of the Deutsche Marine (German Navy); Greece's Dioikisy Ypovrixion Kastrofon (Underwater Demolition Command; DYK), especially noteworthy for their use of the MP5SD; MARCOS, a special-operations unit of the Indian Navy; Indonesia's KOPASKA (short for (Kommando Pasukan Katak, or 'Naval Commando Frogmen'); Malaysia's PASKAL; Poland's Jednostka Wojskowa Formoza (Military Unit Formoza); the Royal Moroccan Gendarmerie; and Singapore's Commando Frogmen, among others. The Vatican Swiss Guard also has MP5s available.

Operators from Poland's Grupa Reagowania Operacyjno-Manewrowego (Operational Maneuver Response Group; GROM) anti-terrorist unit carry out an entry; the point man is using his HK USP pistol and has his HK MP5SD SMG slung. Note that the muzzle of his coverman's MP5 is visible behind and to his left. The point man will often use the pistol to free his other hand for dealing with doors or other obstacles, or to hold an inspection device to peer into rooms. (Author's collection)

IMPACT
An influential SMG

A left-side view of an MP5 produced by EAS in Greece; it has had some alterations, such as installing a different trigger group and the green furniture sometimes encountered on German- or Pakistani-produced MP5s. An interesting feature of the Greek version of the MP5 is the incorporation of a crossbolt, which must be pushed through to allow the SMG's selector to be placed in the full-auto fire position. (C&S)

It might be argued that the most notable impact of the HK MP5 was its contribution to the post-war renaissance of the SMG. During World War II, the SMG had seen substantial use with standard infantry squads, as well as some airborne and special-forces units, not to mention military police and support troops. The Thompson SMG had been popular with US Marines in the Pacific for its close-range striking power, but it was actually heavier than the rifles and carbines in use. The British Sten, of course, had been developed as a cheap, handy weapon when Britain faced the possibility of German invasion, and it served well with airborne and other units. Its replacement, the Sterling, would remain in service with British forces until at least the First Gulf War, but it was primarily used by Military Police, vehicle crews, and other support troops.

In fact, most of the SMGs in use in the early post-war years were those developed during World War II. As a result, the SMGs in use during the Korean War – the Sten, the PPSh-41 and PPS-43, and the US M3 among others – were those that had fought World War II. Prior to the MP5 the

These members of the Royal Malaysian Air Force's PASKAU special-forces unit are armed with a mixture of weapons including a suppressed HK MP5 SMG. EOTech optical sights are used. PASKAU is charged with combat search and rescue as well has hostage rescue aboard hijacked aircraft and other counterterrorist duties. (Author's collection)

most influential SMG of the post-war years was the Israeli Uzi, which was first adopted by the Israeli Army in 1951 and which continues in wide usage today. Designed to arm a citizen army and civilians such as Kibbutzniks, who faced attacks from Arab neighbors, the Uzi proved reliable and easy to handle. Its use of the pistol grip as the magazine well, for example, allowed users to carry out a reload instinctively when stressed. Though the MP5 has always been lauded for its accuracy, it should be noted that Uzi is also quite accurate. The Uzi was eventually adopted by more than 70 countries and is still in use by many. A few other post-war SMG designs are of some note, including the US Ingram, Italian Beretta M12, and Spanish Star Z series. None of these designs achieved anywhere near the success of the Uzi or that of the MP5, however.

A good part of the MP5's success and influence can be attributed to its excellent design, but also to the television crew who filmed the SAS operation at Princes Gate. The cachet of the SAS's success was shared by their primary weapon – the MP5. A few other units influenced by GSG 9 and the SAS had already adopted the MP5, but after Princes Gate, the MP5 became *de rigueur* for elite police and military counterterrorist or special-operations units.

Another noteworthy impact of the MP5 is in the number of countries that have produced licensed copies of the firearm. Among those producing the MP5 are Greece, Iran, Mexico, Pakistan, and Turkey; Sudan produces a version of the MP5 at the Military Industry Corporation using Iranian machinery and designated the Tihraga. Greek and Turkish copies of the MP5 are encountered fairly often in the United States in those police departments that found them less expensive to purchase than those produced by HK. Greek versions were produced first by EBO and more recently at EAS.

An MP5 produced by Pakistan Ordnance Pactory (POF); many users consider the POF MP5 to be of high quality. There are very few obvious differences other than some slight contrast in the color of the furniture and in texture of the pistol grip. (C&S)

Turkish versions are produced by MKEK. One version of the MKEK MP5 achieved a certain amount of success on the US civilian market. The MKEK AT94-A2 9×19mm carbine resembles the HK94 semi-auto carbine that was imported into the United States for a limited time. To qualify as a "carbine" rather than a "short-barreled rifle" under US law, the AT94-A2 has a 413mm barrel. The AT94-A2 retains the closed-bolt, roller-delayed blowback action of the MP5, though with internal changes that limit it to semi-automatic operation. Also, to comply with the laws in some US states, the AT94-A2's magazine well is designed so that it will not take a standard MP5 magazine but instead requires a special ten-round magazine from American Tactical Imports (ATI), the US importer. ATI has also imported MKE 94K pistols, which are semi-auto and retain the short barrel of the "K" model, but do not have a shoulder stock, thus allowing them to be sold as pistols under US law. The 94K pistols are also precluded from taking standard MP5 magazines.

Pakistani versions are made at Pakistan Ordnance Factory (POF). Some seasoned users of the MP5 who have experience with the POF MP5 speak quite highly of it, and in some cases rate it the equal of the HK-produced versions. China also produces a copy, which does not appear to be licensed. Reportedly, some years ago China purchased Pakistani-produced MP5s, which may have provided the basis for the Chinese copies. Chinese copies are produced by Norinco and are designated the NR08.

Saudi Arabia has also produced a licensed version of the MP5 at Military Industries Corporation. Saudi MP5s reportedly use the "S–E–F" trigger group markings but in green rather than red and also have Arabic script on the left side of the receiver. The MP5 is popular with various police and military units in Saudi Arabia. Although the author has not seen the weapons personally, a contact who trained Saudi Royal Guard personnel once mentioned that they had silver- and gold-plated MP5s – silver for enlisted men and gold for officers. Reportedly, these were produced by HK in Germany. Another contact of the author's has also mentioned some gold- and/or silver-plated MP5s in Jordan.

SUCCESSORS

The UMP

Just as HK developed the G36 rifle as a successor to the G3 rifle, the company also developed the UMP as a successor to the MP5. Actually, "successor" may not be the correct word choice, as HK continues to offer the MP5 as well as the UMP. Unlike the MP5, which was designed in Germany, the UMP was designed in the United States by HK USA to meet the demand for an SMG that would chamber the .45 ACP cartridge. To a large extent, the UMP resulted from HK's intent to develop a modular SMG that could be quickly configured to meet an array of missions. As a result of development work in the 1990s, two designs evolved – the MP2000 and the MP5-PIP (Product ImProved). From these weapons, design work began on what would become the UMP, which would be available for sales by mid-1999.

The UMP incorporates some components from the G36 rifle. Features include extensive use of glass-fiber-reinforced polymer parts, with metal inserts when needed. It uses a cold-hammer-forged chrome-lined barrel with the distinctive HK polygonal rifling. While the MP5 uses the HK roller-delayed system, the UMP is a closed-bolt, blowback design. Those used to shooting the MP5 will notice that since the UMP is a blowback design, it does not require the fluted chamber of the MP5, and hence ejected cases do not show the distinctive marks found on ejected MP5 brass. A MIL-STD (military standard) 1913 Picatinny rail is incorporated atop the receiver so that optical sights may be readily mounted. Additional rails may be added to the sides of the receiver or below. Also incorporated are fixed sights – a front post and flip-up rear. The stock, which is well-designed for comfort when firing on full-auto, folds to the side. A quick-connect muzzle interface allows easy attachment of a suppressor; a Brugger & Thomet design is standard. Removal of a locking pin allows the UMP to be stripped into three basic components – upper receiver assembly, lower receiver assembly, and stock. As with the G3 rifle, there is a storage place for the pin in the stock after it has been removed.

Just as the design of the MP5 was based on that of the G3 rifle, that of the UMP was based on the G36 rifle. Shown here is a G36K. The G36 has many interesting features including a combination of two sights – a red dot for close combat and a 3× sight for longer ranges. Its 30-round magazines link together much as those used on the SIG 550 series of rifles. The G36K has proven very popular with special-operations units as it is compact with stock folded, yet offers good range and firepower. (Author)

In addition to .45 ACP (UMP45), the UMP is also chambered for the 9×19mm NATO round (UMP9), and the .40 S&W round (UMP40). Any version may be converted to one of the other chamberings by switching out the barrel, bolt, and magazine. Polymer 30-round magazines are used, holding 30 rounds in 9mm or .40 S&W and 25 rounds in .45 ACP. UMP 9mm magazines are curved, while .40 S&W and .45 ACP magazines are straight. Magazines have a transparent viewing strip to allow the number of rounds remaining to be checked easily. Polymer construction results in the UMP in 9×19mm weighing about 10 percent less than the MP5A2 and about 25 percent less than an MP5A3. With a rate of fire of 650rds/min (in 9×19mm and .40 S&W) versus 800rds/min for an MP5A2 or MP5A3, the UMP is more controllable when fired in bursts. Four trigger-group configurations are available in combinations of safe, single-shot, two-round-burst, and full-auto. There is also a semi-automatic carbine version adopted by some law-enforcement agencies. To aid in controlling the UMP45, cyclic rate was reduced even more, to 600rds/min.

When the last round is fired from a magazine, the UMP bolt locks open. A bolt-release catch on the left side of the UMP allows the support hand to release the bolt after a fresh magazine has been inserted. Likely to appeal to US users, the bolt-release catch is similar to that used on the M4 carbine and M16 rifle. Ambidextrous controls also enhance ergonomics. Although the controls are ambidextrous, they are located in the same positions as for the MP5 to make transitioning simpler. However, since the UMP incorporates the hold-open device mentioned above, when the last round is fired operators familiar with the MP5 will have to adjust their reloading technique to include hitting the bolt release once a fresh magazine has been inserted; magazine insertion is quicker than on an MP5 due to the UMP's flared magazine well. Also, the UMP's controls are designed to be reached easily with shorter fingers.

One characteristic the author noticed in firing the UMP in .40 S&W caliber was that extensive firing on full-auto tended to shatter the bulbs of the standard weapon light, a problem that was alleviated once LED lights came into use. The UMP fired by the author was an early model and this problem has most likely been addressed in later versions. Though the UMP has not achieved the success of the MP5, it has been adopted by more than a dozen countries for use by military or law-enforcement personnel.

The MP7

Another HK weapon which has been produced simultaneously with the MP5 and UMP is the MP7. Normally designated a PDW rather than an SMG, the MP7 has now been in production for more than a decade. The MP7 owes its operating system to the HK G36 short-stroke gas system rather than the blowback operation used on the HK SMGs. It fires with the rotary bolt closed.

Also chambered for a different cartridge than traditional SMGs, the MP7 uses the 4.6×30mm round, which is designed to give excellent penetration of body armor due to its high velocity (735m/sec) and 31-grain bullet with penetrator. In HK military sales materials, it is stated that

OPPOSITE
A Royal Thai Navy SEAL armed with the HK UMP. The UMP has been noted for its durability, with HK advertising the minimum service life of the UMP45 as 100,000 rounds (Gearinger 1999: 47). Not only was its durability intended to be a selling point to US law-enforcement agencies, but also its selling price, which was substantially less than that of the MP5. Due to use of new materials, this reliability does not come at an increase in weight, as the UMP45 weighs about half as much as .45 ACP SMGs of the past (2.5kg versus 3.6kg for the M3A1 or 4.8kg for the M1A1 Thompson). (US Navy)

A blowback, select-fire design, FN's P90 uses a 5.7×28mm cartridge that is very flat shooting, allowing the P90 to be used effectively to 100m or more – and also to penetrate body armor or a ballistic helmet if armor-piercing ammunition is used. A bullpup weapon, it was designed in response to a NATO specification for a compact PDW that was light, had longer range and better penetration than the 9×19mm round, and offered a high magazine capacity. Employing a 50-round magazine that rests atop the receiver, the P90 has a 900rds/min cyclic rate, but is surprisingly controllable given its small size. Although the original version had a telescopic sight – employing a large circle within which is a smaller circle and an aiming dot – other sights are available, as is a flat top to mount an array of optics. The P90 has proven especially popular with elite police and military special-operations units as well as dignitary-protection teams. (Author)

the 4.6×30mm round is designed to defeat the body armor worn by "former Soviet Bloc special forces." It also states that the MP7A1 was developed, in accordance with NATO PDW requirement document D29, to penetrate the CRISAT (Collaborative Research Into Small Arms Technology) vest, comprised of 1.6mm titanium plates and 20 layers of Kevlar, out to 200m and beyond (HK USA n.d.: 7). The MP7/MP7A1 was actually developed to compete with weapons such as FN's P90 PDW rather than conventional SMGs, though it has replaced the MP5 with at least some users.

For lightness, the MP7 is constructed using carbon-fiber reinforced polymers with embedded metal components wherever possible, yet because of the 4.6×30mm cartridge's minimal recoil, it is very comfortable to shoot. It is gas operated and uses a rotating bolt, which is closed when fired. Although it may be used one-handed, its folding stock and vertical foregrip allow it to be used quite effectively with two hands. Ambidextrous selector, magazine release, and bolt release allow ambidextrous use and operation of controls with either hand. The T-shaped cocking handle is centrally located at the rear of the receiver, much like the M4 carbine. As with the Uzi SMG, the magazine well is within the pistol grip and takes 20-, 30-, or 40-round magazines. Some trainers feel that incorporating the magazine well into the grip aids in making a magazine change without looking at the weapon based on the "hand will find hand" principle. A Picatinny rail allows mounting of various optical sighting devices atop the receiver. Adjustable iron sights are designed to be operated through a compact red dot sight if the red dot stops working.

The MP7 has achieved success with some special military and police units, including Austria's EKO Cobra, France's GIGN, Germany's GSG 9, Indonesia's Kopassus, Ireland's An Garda Síochána, Japan's Special Forces Group, the Republic of Korea's 707th Special Mission Battalion, the UK's Ministry of Defence (MOD) Police, and the US Navy SEALs. Note that the UK's MOD Police use the MP7-SF version, which is in semi-automatic configuration. Since the MP7 is used for many of the same missions as the MP5K, a thigh holster has been developed for use by aircrew and a quick-release concealment harness/sling for close-protection teams.

CONCLUSION

The MP5 is an excellent SMG, a point that is difficult to dispute. However, to some extent the success of the MP5 owes a lot to circumstances. The 1972 Munich Olympics massacre jarred many governments awake to the dangers they faced from terrorism, both to citizens and international prestige. As a result, specialized counterterrorist units trained and equipped to deal with hostage situations were formed. Initially, units operated with the weapons and equipment they had available in their own armories, but as the newly formed units trained with their counterparts in other countries and exchanged information, their equipment became more international.

Another fortuitous event for the MP5 was its adoption by West Germany's Bundespolizei and Grenzschutz in 1966. As a result, some German police were actually equipped with the MP5 when the Munich Olympics massacre occurred. The MP5 did not see use, however; Munich police who responded to the incident were, instead, equipped with the Walther MPL. However, when GSG 9, the new German counterterrorist unit – which was part of the Grenzschutz – was formed, the MP5 was among their standard armament. As a result, other European counterterrorist units, including the British SAS, encountered the MP5 and adopted it.

By 1980, when the SAS was called in to end the Iranian Embassy Siege, the MP5 had become the principal weapon in use by its SP Team. Its televised deployment in front of the world soon made the MP5 a vital weapon for counterterrorist, SWAT, and special-operations units around the world. And it was a good choice: very accurate, compact enough to use in tight spaces, reliable, controllable when fired in bursts, and firing a round with limited penetration in buildings, aircraft, ships, and other likely terrorist environments. The MP5 was an excellent "surgical" weapon for many types of mission.

With many units, a carbine such as the US M4, German G36C, or SIG 552 has supplanted the MP5 as units have striven for more stopping power or penetration against subjects wearing body armor. Even with most of those units, however, the MP5 remains in their armories. In some cases it is the MP5K and the MP5SD, which are retained for special circumstances. The MP5K itself has, however, in some units been replaced with FN's P90 or the HK MP7 PDW.

Another market which opened up for the MP5 relatively early in its existence was for a patrol carbine in police vehicles. In countries with a long tradition of police being armed with SMGs, such as Germany, the MP5 quickly became popular. In fact, the use of the shotgun – as in the United States – would have seemed "barbaric," based on German complaints about the applications of combat shotguns by US troops in World War I. Many US law-enforcement agencies adopted the MP5 either in select-fire or semi-auto. Being introduced at a time when more female – and smaller male – police officers were being employed, the MP5 offered an alternative to the traditional 12-gauge "riot" shotguns carried in patrol cars. The MP5 offered more precise shot placement at longer ranges and was far easier to fire. In other countries such as the UK, the "single-shot" or semi-auto version proved a perfect choice for Armed Response Vehicles.

As this book is written, the MP5 is approaching a half-century of service. It still lags behind the Uzi, which is into its seventh decade, but it appears likely the MP5 will continue in use for many more years. In fact, a comparison of the MP5 and the Uzi provides an interesting comment on modern SMG design. The Uzi is not elegant, but it is extremely utilitarian. Designed to arm Israel's citizen army and its security services, the Uzi is renowned for its toughness and basic design. The MP5, on the other hand, is an elegant example of high-precision craftsmanship. Rather than being the weapon of a citizen army, it is the weapon of highly trained special-operations and counterterrorist units. Although the MP5 is renowned for its accuracy, an experienced shooter can do very well with the Uzi, especially the later versions – which also fire from a closed bolt, a design likely influenced by the success of the MP5. Certainly, operators of Israeli elite units such as Sayeret Matkal are capable of using the Uzi with deadly precision.

In some ways, there is a certain continuity to the fact that the German-designed MP5 has achieved such success. After all, the Bergmann MP 18 was the first SMG to see significant combat usage, and during World War II, the MP 38 and MP 40 were among the most innovative and more widely used SMGs. As has been discussed earlier, to some extent, the MP5's dominance among counterterrorist and special-operations units has been lessened by the use of compact rifle-caliber carbines, but it appears likely that the MP5 will continue to serve for many more years. It already ranks among the classic SMGs of all time and that legacy will continue to grow.

BIBLIOGRAPHY

Barnett, Helen (1999). *Urban Warrior: My Deadly Life with the Police Armed Response Unit*. London: Blake.

Camsell, Don (2000). *Black Water: A Life in the Special Boat Service*. London: Lewis International.

Collins, Steve (1997). *The Good Guys Wear Black: The Real-Life Heroes of the Police's Rapid-Response Firearms Unit*. London: Century.

Couch, Dick (2004). *The Finishing School: Earning the Navy SEAL Trident*. New York, NY: Crown Publishers.

Coulson, Danny O. & Elaine Shannon (1999). *No Heroes: Inside the FBI's Secret Counter-Terror Force*. New York, NY: Pocket Books.

Davies, Barry (1994). *Fire Magic: Hijack at Mogadishu*. London: Bloomsbury.

Firmin, Rusty & Will Pearson (2011). *Go! Go! Go!: The SAS, The Iranian Embassy Siege, The True Story*. London: Phoenix.

Gangarosa Jr., Gene (2001). *Heckler & Koch: Armorers of the World*. Accokeek, MD: Stoeger Publishing Co.

Gearanger, Stephen (1999). "HK UMP 45," *Small Arms Review*, February 1999: 43–52.

"George, Jackie" with Susan Ottaway (1999). *She Who Dared: Covert Operations in Northern Ireland with the SAS*. Barnsley: Leo Cooper.

Gray, Roger (2000). *The Trojan Files: Inside Scotland Yard's Elite Armed Response Unit*. London: Virgin.

HK International Training Division (n.d.). *MP-5 Armorers Instruction*.

HK USA (n.d.). *Heckler & Koch Military and Law Enforcement* (catalog). Columbus, GA: Heckler & Koch USA. www.hk-usa.com (accessed June 16, 2013).

HK USA (1993). *Heckler & Koch MP5 Submachine Gun Family Operator's Manual* (draft version). Sterling, VA: Heckler & Koch, Inc.

Hobart, F.W.A. (1973). *Pictorial History of the Sub-Machine Gun*. New York, NY: Charles Scribner's Sons.

James, Frank W. (2000). *Heckler & Koch's MP5 Submachine Gun*. Pahoa, HI: Polynesian Productions.

Jones, Richard D., ed. (2007). *Jane's Infantry Weapons, 2007–2008*. Coulsdon: Jane's Information Group, Ltd.

Kennedy, Michael Paul (1989). *Soldier "I" S.A.S.* London: Bloomsbury.

Marcinko, Richard (1992). *Rogue Warrior*. New York, NY: Pocket Star Books.

Nelson, Thomas B. & Daniel D. Musgrave (1980). *The World's Machine Pistols and Submachine Guns*. Alexandria, VA: TBN Enterprises.

Pugliese, David (2002). *Canada's Secret Commandos: The Unauthorized Story of Joint Task Force Two*. Ottawa: Esprit de Corps Books.

Schatz, Jim (2000). "The New HK MP5F Submachine Gun," *Small Arms Review*, January 2000: 64–68.

Scholey, Pete (1999). *The Joker: 20 Years Inside the SAS*. London: Andre Deutsch.

Scott-Clark, Kathy & Adrian Levy (2013). *The Siege: 68 hours Inside the Taj Hotel*. New York, NY: Penguin Books.

Smith, Stephen (2013). *Stop! Armed Police!: Inside the Met's Firearms Unit*. London: Robert Hale.

Wisdin, Howard E. & Stephen Templin (2011). *SEAL Team Six: Memoirs of an Elite Navy SEAL Sniper*. New York, NY: St. Martin's Press.

Zimba, Jeff W. (2010). "MKE AT-94A2 9mm Carbine," *Small Arms Review*, August 2010: 26–31.

INDEX